Get rich or die tryin'.

That's what this book is about—the good times and the bad times. I wrote this book to explain the world I come from. To a lot of people, I may be too young to reflect on life. And they may be right. But I'd be wasting my blessings if I didn't use the attention I'm getting to shed light on the experiences that have caused me to say the things I say and make the kind of music I make. I want to explain my environment to those who don't come any closer to it than the records they buy or the images they see on television. People want the truth. Even if they can't handle it, they want it. I let you know that I survived nine bullets not to sell records, but because it's the truth. Every time I sit down for an interview, I'm asked, "Well, 50, how did it feel to get shot nine times?" But those stories don't hold the weight, the pain, or the hope of my experience. It just can't. This is my mindset and these are the things that go on. This is why I say the rhymes that I say. This is what happened when I was trying to get rich before I died in Southside Queens.

POCKET BOOKS   MTV BOOKS
New York London Toronto Sydney

FROM
PIECES
TO WEIGHT

50 CENT

Once upon a Time in Southside Queens

This book was written with Kris Ex.

POCKET BOOKS, a division of Simon & Schuster, Inc.
1230 Avenue of the Americas, New York, NY 10020

ISBN-13: 978-0-7434-8804-4
ISBN-10:   0-7434-8804-0

This MTV Books/Pocket Books trade paperback edition September 2006

10 9 8 7 6 5 4 3 2 1

*I dedicate this book to everyone
who has contributed both to my success
and my struggles, as these experiences
lead me to get rich or die tryin'…*

DEDICATION

ACKNOWLEDGMENTS

"You gotta play for tomorrow, even if tomorrow never comes."

Thank you to those who choose to play with the G-Unit . . .

MTV Books and Pocket Books
Interscope Records
Violator Management
Reebok
"Formula 50" Vitamin Water
Jacob & Co.
Paramount Pictures
Vivendi Games
and countless others who execute the vision.

Once upon a Time in Southside Queens

Get rich or die tryin'.

When I say that, everyone focuses on the negative aspects: death, desperation, depression. But you know what? Everybody, from the guy who gets up to punch a clock every day to the kid standing on the corner, is trying to get rich before they die. The guy punching the clock is probably going to night school or has a hustle on the side or some dream he's working on. Why? To get rich. The kid who picks up a bag of drugs to sell is the same way. He's out there in the entrepreneurial spirit, hustling, trying to get rich. That kid just doesn't want to work for anybody—he wants to work for himself. It's just that he has the wrong direction at that point in his life. All at the same time, he's trying to get rich, just like that guy punching a clock, the old man driving a cab, the kid going to college to get his degree, the girl waiting tables at the restaurant. It's all about back to getting rich—or trying to do so. This is nothing new. You can find pretty much the same sentiments in all sorts of philosophies—Samurai codes and shit like that. If Confucius says it, it's wisdom. But when 50 Cent says it, he's being negative.

Either way, it's the truth. I don't necessarily view death as something negative. Death gives meaning to life. Living in fear of death is living in denial. Actually, it's not really living at all, because there is no life without death. It's two sides of the one. You can't just pick up one side and say, "I'm just going to use the 'heads' side." No. It doesn't work like that. You *have* to pick up both sides because nothing is promised to anyone in this world besides death. As soon as a life is created, from the first moment in the womb, it's promised that that life's going to end. Whether it's aborted, stillborn, or the mother has a miscarriage—death's going to come to that life. That's the only guarantee. It doesn't matter if that life goes on to cure every disease ever known or brings about the end of the world as we know it, that life is going to end. You can be sure of that. Death is going to follow life, just like night follows day. It is what it is.

I don't look at death as something to work against; it makes your time here worthwhile. It's what makes life precious. Death provides purpose. It ensures that every situation that comes in life comes for a reason. It's like you have somewhere to go and things to do before you die, and life is always trying to push you to that goal. It's the things we go through that make us who we are. That's why I wouldn't trade my life for anything in this world—I know I have a purpose. The hard times only seemed hard when I was going through them. Now, they're just memories. Besides, if I didn't go through the hard times, I probably wouldn't be able to enjoy the good times.

That's what this book is about—the good times and the bad times. I wrote this book to explain the world I come from. I feel like I have to tell my story while I can. I'm only twenty-nine years old. To a lot of people, I may be too young to reflect on life. And they may be right. But I'd be wasting my blessings and opportunities if I didn't use the attention I'm getting right now to shed light on the experiences that have caused me to think the way I think, say the things I say, and make the kind of music I make. I want to explain my environment to those who don't come any closer to it than the records they buy or the images they see on television. I'm looking back on my life with everything my twenty-nine years has taught me and telling the truth as I see it, while maintaining the honor of the environments that I've come from. I can't share certain information, so I've changed many names and places and identifying details. When I came back to the world of music in 2000, my mission was to tell the truth. Now that I've surpassed my wildest dreams of fame and stardom, that mission hasn't changed.

People want the truth. Even if they can't handle it, they want it. They may want to look at it as a story or music so they can distance themselves from it, but they want it. That's why people watch the news every night. There's nothing good on the news. They'll throw in a little "good news" near the end, like something about a cat being saved from a tree. But before you hear about that cat, you're going to learn that someone got shot and killed, an earthquake killed a couple of hundred people, and that whatever war is going on at the time is still going on and going hard. And you still watch. Why? Because you want the truth. You'll complain, but you'll watch. Every night. The news always gets good ratings.

So I spread my news because no one else is going to do it for me. I let you know that I survived nine bullets not to sell records, but because it's the truth. But it's been turned into a gimmick. Every time I sit down for an interview, I'm asked, "Well, 50, how did it feel to get shot nine times?" Honestly, it didn't feel good—not at the time anyway. Now it's just a memory, but when it happened, it hurt. Bad. I mean it *hurt* hurt—really bad. If you're given a choice, check the box that says "No." It may not seem that bad because it's been packaged into a phrase that you come across in every story about me—"the bullet-riddled rapper who was shot nine times"—but it doesn't hold the weight, the pain, or the hope of my experience. It just can't.

I haven't shown my scars on television to sell records. I haven't let journalists feel the hole in my gum because it sells records. I've shared my reality because these are real situations that happen where I come from. And there are thousands of people who will never get the opportunity to go on TV and tell you what happens in places where gunshots settle arguments. When you look at how my body healed itself, I want you to see the bodies of those who never healed, the ones who didn't make it to the emergency room on time, the ones who never bounced back. That's what I'm the poster child for. And I'd like to be nothing else.

Now that I'm in a totally new environment, when I come around, people get scared, because they feel something bad's going to happen. Every article that you read on me, talks about the possibilities of me being killed, or me killing somebody. It makes people uneasy when I'm around. But I'm just as uncomfortable being around the people that I am around now as they are being around me. I don't know whether they were sent to be a writer, a photographer, or if they're a federal agent. It's a simple fact that when white people pop up in my neighborhood, they're usually there to take us to jail. I definitely don't have anything against white people, but in that environment, when we see them, the first thing we look to think is, "Are they police?" Once we realize they're not the police, they're cool with us. And probably in their environments, they see us and they look and think, "Are they up to something?" And then after they figure out that we're not up to anything, we're alright with them. It's the same shit. Being racist and being realistic are two different things.

Sometimes the only way I can understand things is to put them in a negative or street connotation. If I can make an analogy for a situation to what it would be on the street, then I can understand it real easy. Gradually, I'll become something different. I'm going to different places, I'm seeing different things, moving in different circles—I'm becoming a broader person. My outlook on the world is changing, but it hasn't totally changed. Change takes time. I've only been out of the 'hood for a few years, so those experiences outweigh the new ones. There are many more memories trying to get rich than there are of being rich. I can't forget what made me who I am. That's my struggle, and I think that's everyone's struggle, too. We have to learn from the lessons life gives us and put them to good use while we have the time because no one is promised tomorrow.

In my head and in my heart I know that when it's my time to go, I'm going to go. I may die tomorrow, but that only makes me work harder today. In many ways, I've already won; I've already exceeded the expectations that people had of me. I've defied the odds. I wasn't supposed to win. I'm from the bottom. But I overcame the obstacles that were in front of me. And for a moment, I got to feel what it feels like for the world to focus on me—for being a winner. No one can take that away from me. Just like they can't take away what came before. Now there are people who would actually like to be me. But if they had to go through the situations I was in before I became a rap star, I don't think they'd still want to be me.

People already have a perception of me. When I meet them, they think, This guy's crazy. But you have to look at it and realize, This is how they think in the 'hood. This is my mind-set and these are the things that go on. This is why I say the rhymes that I say. This is what happened when I was trying to get rich before I died in Southside Queens.

*"There was no
such thing as crack..."*

I can remember when there was no such thing as crack. Sure, there were ways to get high. Everybody used the old standby: Pot, grass, weed, herb, cheeba, chronic, trees, indo, doja—whatever they called it then, whatever they call it now, and whatever they'll call it in the future, it was marijuana; it was an escape, a portable vacation.

There was heroin, which came from morphine, which came from opium. Opium was around before Jesus. It was big in Asia, Europe, and the Middle East—they used it as medicine. Morphine hasn't been around as long. It was made as a painkiller at the beginning of the nineteenth century by a German physician who named it after Morpheus, the Greek god of dreams. In Vietnam War movies, when a soldier gets all shot up, he'll be in some serious pain—breathing all heavy, telling the guy holding his hand to make sure that his mom or girlfriend or whoever gets his last letter and the little heart he had been making for her out of wood or whatever it is. The guy holding the shot soldier's hand will scream, "Doc! We need more morphine!" Then the medic runs over and shoots the guy with a needle dose of the stuff. (I remember in one film, the commander just shot the guy in a mercy killing because they needed to save the morphine, but that's beside the point.) After the guy gets the morphine, that's it. No more pain. He goes all peaceful, right into the arms of Morpheus. I guess heroin really cranked up the dream-god factor, because all I've ever seen it do is make people nod off like walking zombies.

Cocaine's been around for a long time, too. But it hasn't always been treated the way that it's treated today. In 1863, Italians used cocaine to make a wine that even the pope loved so much that he raved about its ability to "spark the divinity of the soul," or something like that. Twenty years later, Sigmund Freud, the father of modern psychology, called coke "magical" and couldn't get enough of the stuff—he didn't even stick to the wine. He went for the raw white—snorted it, injected it, painted it on his skin. At the time, cocaine was a wonder drug, a stimulant and painkiller that cured everything from impotency to masturbation and was used as a surgical anesthetic. (There were even ads with children in them for fifteen-cent cocaine tooth drops: "An Instantaneous Cure!") Some guy started making the wine in Atlanta, but then Prohibition came around, so he took out the alcohol and renamed it Coca-Cola. Somewhere along the line, around the start of the twentieth century, cocaine was deemed illegal and became a serious problem. But it was still available if you knew the right people.

All of these things and more were in place when my grandparents Curtis and Beulah Jackson moved to South Jamaica, Queens, from Ackerson, South Carolina. But there was no such thing as crack. That came later.

Back then, Queens, which is big enough to be America's fifth-largest city, was a haven for relatively successful blacks. Harlem, New York City's original Negro mecca, was deteriorating under the pressure of all the blacks who were coming up from the South and seeking opportunity in the big city. The former slaves decided to spread out from their little corner of New York, past lower Manhattan (which even then was too expensive for most people), and rested across the water, underneath the trees growing in Brooklyn. But then Brooklyn itself became too near to the madness of the inner-city strife. So it was that Queens emerged as home to some pretty notable Negroes. In the earliest part of the twentieth century, there was Lewis Latimer, the inventor who expanded on the lightbulb created by his former mentor, Thomas Edison, by creating and patenting the carbon filament. Later, in the 1950s, Queens was home to jazz legends like John Birks "Dizzy" Gillespie, Louis Armstrong, Ella Fitzgerald, William "Count" Basie, and baseball giant Jackie Robinson. Queens is just a stone's throw away from Brooklyn (which is also known as Kings County), and the only things separating the two places are the man-made lines on a map, but Queens is built much differently than Brooklyn. Because it's farther into the mainland, it was settled and laid out in an easier, more suburban fashion than Brooklyn and Manhattan, which were basically laid out as grids. Queens' villagelike landscape, low bridges, and lack of public-transportation services made it the great escape for those who wanted easy access to the big city without the dangers of full-time residence in the core of the Rotten Apple.

My grandparents had nine children: Curtis Jr., Geraldine, Cynthia, Jennifer, Harold, Johnny, Karen, and Sabrina, my mom. By the time my mom was born, in 1960, Queens began to soil. It was no longer the quick retreat from urban squalor. In 1964, the borough became the focus of the country, not only for hosting the World's Fair and the opening of Shea Stadium but for what happened to Catherine "Kitty" Genovese. She was murdered. Two and a half miles from my grandparents' home, she was stabbed seventeen times with a hunting knife over the course of a half hour as thirty-eight people watched from their homes. After this, the city created the 911 emergency response system and increased the number of white people who were moving to Long Island's Nassau and Suffolk counties because of all the blacks coming in. That's the Queens I know. All the other stuff I remember from school or read in magazines, when people write about the place where I grew up.

To hear my mom tell it, when she was fifteen years old—on July 6, 1975, to be exact—the impossible happened, and she gave birth to me via immaculate conception, just like Mary did with Jesus. She named me Curtis James Jackson III, in honor of her father, but called me Boo-Boo (the one and only true Curtis Jackson was and still remains my grandfather; even Curtis Jr., my uncle, had to take to being called Star). Whenever I asked my mom about my dad, she would say, "You don't have a father. I'm your mama *and* your daddy."

Even though I didn't know what that meant, I knew what it meant. If you were a kid growing up in my neighborhood, it was weird for you to have both parents around. You either got one parent or you got grandparents. I had one parent and two grandparents. From what I could tell, I was actually ahead of the game. And when it came time to bring it— whether "it" was love, money, or authority—my mom would bring it. That's the only thing that mattered to me.

I remember seeing my mom hanging out with women more than she hung out with men. She had this one friend named Tammy who would always be around, so one time I asked my grandmother, "Why does Ma always come around with Tammy?" My grandmother said, "That's something you should ask your mother about." And then I dropped the subject. I was young, but I wasn't stupid. I learned early on that when it came to my mom, there were things you talked about and things that you didn't.

My mom was, in a word, *hard*. She was real aggressive. As a disciplinarian, she was stern. As a motivator, she was even harsher. She encouraged me to do things that I knew I couldn't do if she didn't have my back. Once, when I was about five years old, I came running into my grandmother's house, crying, because I had been fighting with some kids up the block.

We had been shooting marbles when this kid missed a really easy shot and I laughed at him. He must've been having a bad day because he got real upset and wanted to fight. Because he was much bigger than me, all the other kids got on his side to beat me up. I was like, You can't be serious. This kid was already bigger than the legal size for five-year-olds. He was so big that, on principle alone, he should have been eight or nine. If we were in a boxing league, he would have been at least three weight classes above me. It's not like he needed the help. So I did the only thing I could: I took my ass-whupping and went home to cry.

When I got home, my mom was pissed. She asked, "What the hell are you crying about?"

I explained it to her. "There was this boy," I told her, "he's as big as a whole block, maybe two. He beat me up and he wasn't quite finished with me when I ran, so if it's all the same to you, I'll be spending the rest of my fifth year in the house."

My mom asked where he was. I said, "He's still outside, blocking out the sun, most likely. You can't fight him, Ma." She looked at me like I had left my common sense on the street. I don't know if she was shocked that I thought she'd fight my battle for me or just disappointed in me for running. She said, "Go back out there and fight him again. If you get your ass beat again, you're gonna take it without crying."

I would have sworn that something was wrong with my ears. Or maybe hers. I said, "Ma, this kid is big. Like, *big* big."

"I don't care if he's bigger than you," she said. "You pick something up and hit him with it if you have to. But you're not going to come back in here crying."

It wasn't really a hard decision at that point. The worst the kid I was fighting could do was to kill me. But I was more scared of my mom at that moment. I went back out there, picked up a rock that I could barely hold in my hand, and I knocked the fuck out of that kid with it. It was the first time I ever hit someone hard enough to make him go down. He was curled up on the floor bleeding and saying that he was going to tell his mother on me. But I didn't care. His mom could only go and talk to my mom, and I had a strong feeling that any confrontation between our mothers would end up much like the one between him and me did. "So what?" I screamed. "Go tell your mother. She can get hit, too!"

All the kids started egging the fight on. "Ooooh! He talked about your momma!" I told them to shut up or they could get hit, too. They shut up. And that kid never came back with his mother. In fact, he never bothered me again.

That's what it was like when I was with my mom. I felt like I could do anything as long as I had her consent. But she wasn't around much. She had moved out of my grandparents' house when I was a little baby and left me with them. But every time I saw her, she would have something for me. Every visit was like Christmas. If there wasn't a toy, clothing, or a piece of jewelry, there was cold, hard cash. When I was six, she got me a children's dirt bike. It was obviously secondhand, but it was clean and came with a brand-new helmet. By that time, I began to pick up that she was selling drugs, so I knew she had probably taken it from someone who couldn't afford to pay what she wanted in cash. I didn't care. It actually made the bike seem like more than it was because I knew she was thinking about me when she was working. And, shit, it was new to me. In my eyes, I had a *new* bike. Actually, I had a *motorcycle*. I was like, What? You mean I don't have to waste time pedaling around and around to move? Oh, it's on. All I needed was a quarter or two for some gas and I could ride all day. My mom had a real, grown person's dirt bike and she even allowed me to ride alongside her in the street. Where most mothers would say, "No, you can't do that because you're going to hurt yourself," she said. "Don't be scared. You can do it. The worst thing you could do is hurt yourself and nothing that hurts can last too long." Whenever she came around, we would be zipping down the street.

The bike was small enough to fit through the front door of my grandmother's house, so I would take it inside and spend my time wiping it down, shining the spokes and everything, until it came time for me to ride it again. I cleaned that bike a lot because there were many days when I didn't have any gas money, and, sometimes, when I had the money, I couldn't find anyone to take me down to the gas station. There may have been eight aunts and uncles in the house, but most of them were still in their teens and they didn't look at me like I was their responsibility.

With that many kids in the house, the resources that most kids take for granted were at a premium. There seemed to be just enough of everything to go around, but there never seemed to be enough *good* stuff to go around. There was enough food, but not enough of the fun food that was shown on TV, the food that made life a good place to live, the food that made you nothing if you couldn't get it. There was enough clothing to go around, but not enough clothing that hadn't been worn before by someone else, not enough clothing that hadn't been washed to within a thread of its existence, not enough clothing with the types of tags and pictures that kept the other kids from laughing at you. There was enough plastic and buckets to go around, but not enough plastic to keep out the chill of winter when it bit through the house, not enough buckets to catch the tears of the house when it cried because the rain had been too much for it to bear.

But there was always somebody around, and that meant that there was always somebody's business I could get into. I was a nosy kid, and as a reward for my inquisitiveness, I would be quickly banished from the vicinity of anything worth eavesdropping on: "Stay outta grown folks' business. Go upstairs." I was always the nigga upstairs. I got to know upstairs real well—me and my little green army men. I used to talk to them like they were real people. "They always making us go upstairs," I'd say. And my army men would reply, "That's 'cause they're stupid. They're not as smart as we are. We could have more fun without them." "You know what? I think you're right." When I started to go to school by myself, I wasn't by myself. I was with my army men. There was this big dog that I used to be scared of because every time I walked by it, the dog would come to the gate, barking like it wanted to eat me. I just talked to my army men. "Don't be scared of that dog. That dog isn't gonna do nothing. I'll whup that dog if he comes out that gate." That's how I talked myself into not being afraid of the dog. I used to walk around with one of my army men and tell him not to be afraid of things, and then I started acting like the things I was telling the man. "Look, I'm not afraid of the dog. I'll show you." Then I'd kick the gate and run. "See, I told you I wasn't scared."

Sometimes my aunts would throw dollar parties in the backyard, where they charged their friends one dollar to come into the backyard and party. It didn't make sense to me, because they would have people in the backyard at other times and they never charged anyone. But once they threw on some music and put out some food, the same people who ate in the house for free any other day of the week would pay to get past the gate. Those parties were my earliest experiences in marketing. They were also the first time I got to see how hip-hop affected people. A lot of times, they played old soul grooves and everyone just played it real cool. But when a hip-hop song came on, the party really got jumping. The guys would all start rapping with the music, and the girls would break out into little dance routines. There would always be a few guys who were really into it, who would start pop-locking and break dancing. I would just watch from the upstairs window and think about when I'd be old enough to throw my own parties. I figured that I'd be able to keep all the money for myself and make even more money than my aunts, because they had to split it four ways.

When I was about seven, my mom would come and take me for a day while she was conducting her business. She had an apartment on top of a storefront on Old South Road, right on the other side of Baisley Pond Park. This was the first time that I actually saw her dealing drugs. I had already figured it out by the things she was buying for me, but I had never seen her actually working. All the people who came around her were either customers or dealers. It didn't take me long to tell who was who. The dealers were mostly older men who drove nice, big cars like Cadillac DeVilles and Fleetwood Broughams, with big rectangular grilles behind the gleaming metal fenders, clean down to the whitewall tires, or Pontiac Bonnevilles, with lush velour interiors that made the drivers seem as if they were cruising from the inside of a pillow. The dealers were always crisp, down to their starched collars and freshly pressed slacks. They would drive up, hop out of their shining cars, their clothes glowing, their jewelry glistening, and their hair perfectly sculpted. The customers were the guys who came up to them, usually walking.

I was amazed at how my mom talked to the guys with the big

cars. They treated her like she was their equal. I had never seen anything like it. When they saw her, they would compliment her and speak in some code I couldn't figure out. Then they'd give her a brown paper bag and she'd give them a fat stack of cash. When I got back to my grandmother's house, I would tell my uncles about it. They'd just laugh and tell me that the guys on South Road were *getting it.* "You got some cats getting it over here," they would say. "But not like on South Road. They're really getting it over there."

Uncle Harold told me that there was a man named Big Tony who lived not too far from the house who was getting it. He said that Big Tony was getting it so well that people had stopped calling him Big Tony, and now just about everyone called him Godfather. I couldn't believe it. What I had seen on South Road was too different from anything that I had seen on our side of the park. But when Harold told me that Godfather was the guy who drove around in a big, green Lincoln Continental and bought ice cream for everyone when the truck came around, I knew who he was talking about. Harold must have seen that I was impressed because he said, "Don't worry, when I'm *getting it,* I'm gonna make sure to take care of my little nephew."

I still wasn't exactly sure what *it* was or how they got it, but I wanted *it* more than I wanted to throw parties in the backyard or play with my army men. And the more time I spent on South Road, the more I figured out that *getting it* meant that you could stay up late on any night of the week. I knew that the people who weren't *getting it* had to go to bed early so they could disappear to work. When my mom came to pick me up in her new car—a black Buick Regal with a white vinyl top—I was sure that *getting it* was the only way to go.

But even with all that, I never liked spending the night at my mom's house. It was nice there, but the environment was different and I felt lonely there. It got worse when she got a house out on Long Island. It was more peaceful there, and that was the problem. I had become so accustomed to the constant party that was my grandmother's house. My aunts and uncles may not have been the most nurturing people in the world, but at least there was always someone's goings-on I could stick my nose into. At my grandmother's house, I could fall asleep on the couch and there would be someone around, talking on the phone or watching TV. My mom's house was so solitary that the silence made me uncomfortable. After I was there for a while, I'd say, "I wanna go home. Take me back to Grandma's house." And she would.

After she moved to Long Island, my mom's visits grew so sporadic that I can't honestly recall the last time I saw her. The last clear memory I have is of her showing up at Aunt Karen's wedding. It was at this small church next to a gas station off of Linden Boulevard. I remember that my mom put some money in my pocket and we took some pictures together. Those are the last pictures my family has of her.

///////,,,,,,,//////

To this day, my grandfather is a man who speaks his feelings freely and without any fear of retribution. He doesn't mean to hurt anyone's feelings, but he says exactly what's on his mind, thinking without considering how his words will affect anyone. He had raised nine children and provided for them to the best of his ability, so his attitude was, "I don't give a fuck who thinks what. You can leave. You don't like it, you can get outta my house. This is what I put together. You motherfuckers can go."

My grandfather isn't the type of guy who wears emotion on his face. He just has this permanent scowl. If you looked through a strong-enough microscope and measured with instruments that are used to tell the length of a fly's wings, you could probably see that the corners of his mouth turn upward when he gets really, really happy. When he's upset, he looks just like he looks at any other moment. The only time I ever saw my grandfather outside of his normal range of emotion was when he found out that my mom had been murdered.

Seeing my grandfather cry was like watching one of those horror movies where a statue or a painting comes to life. I was like, that's not supposed to happen. That was what freaked me out even before my grandmother told me that my mom wasn't going to be coming back and that I'd be staying at their house permanently. She didn't explain much about what happened at the time. She didn't have to. Even at eight years of age you know what it means when you hear that your mother isn't coming back. It meant that Christmas was over.

"There was always drama . . ."

Stupid shit. That's the best way to explain what I found myself going through, getting into and doing for the first few years after my mother died. Not anything extravagantly stupid, just garden-variety stupid shit like using the downstairs window as an exit from the house when there was a perfectly good front door available. Or climbing over the short chain-link fence as opposed to swinging open the gate like a normal human being. Stupid shit like getting into fights with kids at school three days of the week or telling teachers what they could do with their lesson plans and homework assignments. Stupid shit like dashing and darting through the house like some sort of windup toy that could not be unwound. That is, until someone suggested that I be put on methylphenidate, otherwise known to hyperactive children around the world as Ritalin.

The Ritalin worked, not necessarily because the medicine was effective but because it's as potent as any drug ever administered to a child. The logic of the medical establishment to introduce a stimulant to a hyperactive system paid off: With each dose, I could feel every blood vessel in my head swell up and I would become woozy. I slowed down, looking and feeling like a dope fiend to the point where I began to slow myself down rather than take the medicine full-time. It became a threat: "Slow down or I'll give you your medication."

"All right, I'll be good."

In my head, the reason things were going bad for me was because my mom wasn't around. This was my rationalization for all things, big or small. When my aunt was getting on my nerves, I knew it wouldn't be going down like that if my mom were around. If I got yelled at for dragging mud through the house, I'd think, I wouldn't be getting punished if my mom were here. Even if it was raining, I'd sit there looking out the window, thinking that only if my mom were around, the sun would be out. Every time I had seen my mom, something good would happen. But then I couldn't see her anymore. And nothing seemed to go right. Someone had even stolen the bike she had given me. That really fucked me up. I just woke up one morning, went outside, and it was gone. Just like my mom.

My grandmother picked up on what I was going through, probably before I did, because she showered me with *extra* extra love and seemed to give me more leeway than she had ever given any of my aunts and uncles. I knew this much because my youngest aunt, Cynthia, never passed up an opportunity to point out that I was receiving an excessive amount of pardons. Cynthia and I were damned-near mortal enemies. My battles with Cynthia began immediately after the grief surrounding my mother's death rolled away, leaving her with a clear view of the new family portrait. She quickly realized that the position she had cherished as the baby of the family was no longer hers—it was mine.

Being the youngest of the nine children meant that Cynthia was already saddled with the house grunt work. But to her, the added responsibility of watching me after school wasn't a chore, it was an opportunity for revenge. She was very passive-aggressive with her torture. She never really came right out and fucked with me. All she did was follow my grandmother's instructions to the letter. For instance, I'd be watching TV and she'd say, "Grandma said you can't watch any TV until you did your homework."

"I finished my homework," I'd say, plopping in front of the set.

"Well, I have to check it first," she'd say. Then she'd shut the TV off right in front of me! She did things like that on purpose. She would allow me to watch just enough of a show to whet my appetite, then, usually just about the time that the major action was about to take place, she would flick off the set and order Boo-Boo to do his homework. She knew damn well that the only afternoon cartoons worth watching came on between 3:00 and 4:30 P.M. Even if I did my homework quick enough to catch anything worth watching, she'd take her sweet time before getting around to checking my homework.

The thing is, Cynthia was a nerd that loved homework and anything to do with it, so it wasn't like checking my homework put her out of her way. To her it was like, Great! I get to torture my nephew and do schoolwork at the same time! She even had the thick bifocal glasses to prove it. And it was those glasses that allowed me to exact a small dose of vengeance after she killed Dillinger.

To this day, Cynthia will swear on a truckload of Bibles that she had nothing to with the death—heck, *murder*—of my second dog. The first one had been hit by a car in the street, so I'm almost sure she had nothing to do with that. But Dillinger was a different story. The Doberman pinscher was a gift to both the family and me. Even with the threat of Ritalin, I was out of control. No adult or child in the house could keep up with me, and none wanted to. A dog was the best way anyone could think of to give me some company and keep my hands full. I loved that dog. He slept in my bed with me even after he grew so big that he scared the rest of the family. Dillinger made everyone nervous because they thought he was mean. He was cool with me, but he didn't get along too well with anyone else.

The only problem I had with Dillinger was that the dog was greedy. He was a dog that would eat one hundred times a day regardless of what was put in front of him. He had started out easily enough on dry dog food, but when I began to give him the table scraps that I didn't want, the dog got in his head that human food wasn't off-limits. Problem. It wasn't long before Dillinger would jump up on the table and go for the food right on my dinner plate. That's when he really started to scare my family, and they began to mutter about getting rid of him. I tried to play it off as if everything was copacetic, but no one was hearing it. They said, "A dog ain't supposed to jump up on the table like that."

I tried to talk to the dog: "Look, if you keep jumping on the table, they're gonna get rid of you." Disciplining Dillinger was out of the question. There was no way I could control him. So I began to feed him as much as I could after school, when no one was around. The only thing that came of that was that the dog began to snatch food right out of my hand whenever I ate. I could be eating a sandwich, and he'd rip it right out of my hand, just barely missing a finger. But things really got out of hand when Dillinger ate the Thanksgiving turkey one year.

My grandmother always precooked the Thanksgiving turkey on Wednesday, so that she could concentrate on the fixings, trimmings, and side dishes on Thursday. When I was ten, she made the mistake of leaving the fully cooked, juicy, family-sized turkey on the kitchen table to cool off overnight. The next morning when I came down to feed Dillinger, he was cleaning off the bones of the turkey. I couldn't believe it. I knew right then that Dillinger's days were numbered. But I still didn't expect Cynthia to kill him.

She was real slick about it. She used his own greed against him and let him do most of the work. All she did was fill up a bowl with roach spray so it looked like milk, and placed the bowl on the floor. Of course, any normal dog would have some sense of self-preservation that would have kept it from drinking a bowl of poison. Not Dillinger. He went right at it. I think that when he died, his only regret was that he didn't get to finish his last meal.

I knew that Cynthia did it on purpose. She said she didn't put it there for him. But why else would you fill a bowl with roach spray? But I was the only friend Dillinger had in the house, so all my pleas fell on deaf ears. I set revenge on the back burner, knowing that an opportunity would present itself. When it did, I would act swiftly. That's all there was to it.

My chance came one Sunday morning when I was going through the coupons in the newspaper. When I came across a page of Christmas stamps, the idea hit me so fast it felt like it was always there. I raced upstairs, crept into Cynthia's bedroom, and snatched the bifocals she kept on her night table. I ran back downstairs and applied every last stamp to her lenses and put the glasses back on the night table. Then I waited. . . .

"Aaaaaaaaaahhhhhhhhh!!!!!!!!!" Cynthia was screaming. "Aaaaaa-aaahhhhhhhhh!!!!!!!!!" She was crying so loud I got scared. I thought that she might have hurt herself. Then I heard, "Ma! Help! Maaaaaaaaaa!"

I heard my grandmother run into the room as Cynthia cried, "Maaaaaaaa! Help!!! I'm blind!!!!!!!" Then my grandmother began to laugh.

I ran upstairs and saw Cynthia looking around the room through the colorful glasses but unable to see a thing, crying, "I'm blind!"

I didn't even take into account that Cynthia was in the habit of not opening her eyes until she had her bifocals in place. I just wanted to inconvenience her, but she helped take my little scheme to the next level. She actually thought that she was blind! Oh man, that was priceless.

Cynthia was more embarrassed from thinking she was blind than she would have been from actually losing her sight. And it got worse because my grandmother retold the tale for every family member and visitor who happened to miss the event. It was like I got to relive the event all over again each time I heard the story. *Hey, Mr. Mailman, did you ever hear about the time my aunt thought she was blind? No, well my grandmother would love to tell you all about it. Come inside and have a seat. You're going to love this.*

//////,,,,,,,//////

Growing up, there was always drama in my house. Most of my aunts and uncles were getting high, getting drunk, or a combination of the two. Even my grandfather used to get drunk. My grandmother didn't like it, but there wasn't much she could do about it. I remember one summer night not too long after Uncle Johnny had come back from the navy and everyone was drinking in the backyard. I don't know if Uncle Johnny had picked up his drinking problem in the navy or if he had fallen into it when he came back home, but he was well and drunk the night he burned off his hands.

My grandfather was out there with his friends. Uncle Johnny was out there with Uncle Harold, Uncle Star, and a few of their friends. As the night wound down and the bottles got low, the old-timers and the young bucks started making all sorts of shit-talking challenges to each other. Uncle Star was reliving his glory days as a basketball player. It didn't seem to bother him that no one could recall him playing well in any game at any time, let alone breaking all the records he was claiming. "I was the best in the park, man," he said. "Why you think Daddy named me Star?" My grandfather said that it was because *he* was the only Curtis in the family, but if Star wanted to be called Curtis, he'd gladly fight him for the name.

Then one of my grandfather's friends said to Uncle Johnny, "I bet you can't move that ice from right there to over here," pointing to a steaming block of dry ice that they had been using to keep the drinks cold.

"I bet you I can too move that block of ice," said Johnny.

"Well, we're betting that you can't."

Johnny walked over to the ice, popping shit about having been in the navy and all the things he did—moving a block of ice was *nothing*. Even I knew better than to go over to that ice. But not Johnny. He bent down to grab the ice by the sides and burned off all the skin on his forearms. My grandmother had to drive him to the hospital because she was the only one sober enough to get behind the wheel that night.

That's the type of crazy shit I grew up around. It happened so much that it seemed normal. I thought that everybody's family sat around, got drunk, and played practical jokes that caused second-degree burns.

"What part of the game is this?"

Despite the madness that went on in my house, I tried to have a pretty normal upbringing. I'd play street football games, two-handed touch style, with the sewers marking the goalposts. But I didn't really like playing football, or any other team sport, for that matter. With team sports, the other kids would drop the ball or mess up a play and we'd lose the game. I hated that shit. Even back then, the idea of not being in control of my own destiny, even if only for a game, made me uncomfortable.

I spent a lot of time alone, fantasizing about having things I couldn't afford. I'd spend whole days looking at the cars passing by: "That's my car!" I don't know any kid or anyone who was a kid who didn't play that game. I think it's a normal thing for a young kid to play with a toy car while dreaming of having the real thing. But when I saw one and said, "That's my car," I really meant it. I wanted *that* car, the one I really saw. And I didn't want any other car. When I got it in my head that I was going to drive a Mercedes-Benz, that was it. I knew I was going to do it. That's what was in my mind and that's what it was going to be in reality. I got a small toy Benz and I carried it around in my pocket, as if I could make the real thing manifest by pure will.

It's not like I was having idle visions. The older guys that I had seen around my mom all drove big American cars and wore flashy suits with expensive shoes. But around the time I was ten, I began to see a change in who had the money, power, and respect in the neighborhood. The new generation was full of teens who drove smaller foreign cars like Benzes, BMWs, Audis, and Saabs. They wore tracksuits with brand-new sneakers and draped themselves in the biggest, chunkiest pieces of gold they could afford.

CHAPTER 3

Sincere was one of the new breed. His aunt lived next door to my grandmother's house and his grandfather lived two blocks away. He was practically family. Sometimes he'd see me in the street doing nothing. My sneakers would be torn; my clothes dirty; and my skin ashy. He'd pop open the door to his BMW and, just like that, he'd take me shopping. And not just around the corner but down to Jamaica Avenue to the mall, to Pop's, where he'd get me Fila sweatsuits and all sorts of sneakers: Ellesses, Lottos, Adidas, Nikes. When it was cooler outside, he got me a Starter jacket. It was big because the things that he got me actually matched one another—it wasn't just what was on sale. In Brooklyn, people were getting robbed and killed for these things; I was getting them for free. I'd even wear the stuff he got me inside the house, where there was no one to see me. Because my grandmother didn't get the clothes for me, she couldn't tell me to take off anything or to save it for a "special occasion."

My grandmother did her best for me, but she had already fed a lot of mouths. When she raised her kids, sneakers cost a couple of dollars. Back then, even the good brand-name ones cost about twenty dollars. But the sneakers I wanted were going for fifty dollars easily, and the really fly ones were damn near a hundred dollars. That didn't make any sense to her. To her, fifty dollars was a good winter coat and some slacks, not a pair of sneakers. How was I supposed to ask her for a pair of Air Jordans costing a buck and change with a straight face? I couldn't do it.

My aunts and uncles couldn't have been any tighter with money if they had been wrapped with rubber bands. If I asked them for money, it was like I insulted them: "Five dollars? For what? You want to 'borrow' or you want me to *give* you five dollars? Don't be asking me for no money."

The only one who ever looked out for me was Uncle Harold. He had married a Haitian woman named Sharon, whose family was moving lots of marijuana and cocaine from Mexico through the Southwest. In exchange for taking their sister off their hands, my uncle's new brothers-in-law set him up in the business. It wasn't long before he was doing well enough to buy a house in Miami and keep a place to work out of in Houston. Before he moved to Miami full-time, he bought me a scooter to replace the one that had been stolen from me.

Aunt Karen's husband, Uncle Trevor, did little things for me, and he wasn't even a blood relative. Trevor always had something for me every time we crossed paths. His crew of Jamaicans was notorious. I didn't know much about them when I was younger, but I saw that the guys I thought were something would be on their p's and q's whenever Trevor or his people were around. I didn't understand it; in my eyes, Uncle Trevor was just a nice guy who made some money and shared it with the people around him. Even after Trevor got locked up and was sentenced to thirteen years, I never saw him as a bad person. One time, he went so far as to get my grandmother a brand-new 190E Mercedes-Benz, because her Oldsmobile was always breaking down. This was back in 1985, when that Benz was like "fuckin' wow!" My grandfather and I started talking shit like, "Why *she* get a car?"

These were the only people I ever saw who were able to do anything for anyone outside of themselves—and they were all hustling drugs. All of the hustlers were generous—except for my cousin, Brian. He never gave anyone a damned thing. Sincere was the main one who looked out for me. When I was with him, I saw that everyone treated him with respect. The store owners greeted him like family, and all the hustlers looked up to him. I liked the feeling I got when I was with Sincere. There was no way you could tell me that hustling was a bad thing. These were the people I saw as I grew up. They were my role models.

At this point, back in the early half of the eighties, cocaine was a recreational drug. My aunts and uncles—Star, Johnny, and Jennie (who had come back worse off from the army than when Johnny had returned from the navy)—used coke. They'd get together with their friends, sniff some lines, and go out. When they came back, they'd hit a few more lines and drink till they went to sleep the next afternoon. I'd wake up in the morning from all the loud talking and find them in the living room with the same clothes they had on when I went to sleep. They'd be having such a good time that when they ran out of coke, no one would want to go get more, so they'd send me down the block to Brian's house for Fat Alberts. A Fat Albert was about a quarter gram of cocaine, wrapped in aluminum foil or a shred of a plastic bag, that sold for twenty-five dollars. Brian was only in high school. Actually, he was at the age when he should have been in high school, but I never saw him doing homework or carrying books. When I saw him, he was clean-cut and freshly dipped. He hung out with guys who were much older and drove a whitewall-tired Pontiac Bonneville. But like I said, even though he was my cousin, he never gave me anything.

One time, I had fifty dollars in my pocket and was picking up some Alberts from Brian. He had on a brand-new pair of sneakers, and about six or seven boxes of kicks he hadn't even worn yet were stacked in the bedroom. It was one of the craziest things I had ever seen. It looked like a corner in one of the sneaker stores Sincere took me to. I asked Brian if he would buy me a new pair of sneakers, because the ones I had were all worn out. I showed him the bottom of my Lottos. A torn sock and the head of my naked big toe were sticking out like, "Hello." This nigga Brian laughed at me, counted the money I had given him, handed me the two Alberts, and sent me on my way. I was like, fuck that. After that, I never went back to Brian to pick up anything. From then on, I went to see Sincere.

But the time came when Sincere wouldn't buy clothes or sneakers for me, either. Sincere began to change. Mel and Jack, some of the older guys from the neighborhood, had kidnapped his grandfather for ransom money. Mel and Jack were the same guys who specialized in robbing banks for money. The times were changing, but guys like this refused to change with them. They lacked the finesse and patience the drug game required, so they stuck to their strong-arm tactics. "Takeover"—that's what they called it. Broad-daylight raids—everyone down on the fucking floor—bitch, open up the safe. They'd almost always go for the vault cash, because that's where the real money was; the money from the tellers was small peanuts, and it was often marked. The money in the back may or may not have been registered by serial number, but it was a better return on the risk of having the guards, customers, and employees facedown at gunpoint, like it was still the Al Capone days. And then they started getting high, like they weren't crazy enough already.

Sincere told me that I had to keep my mouth shut about things like this. He didn't even have to tell me that because I was freaked out by the whole thing. I was like, "What part of the game is this?" That shit made no sense to me. I asked Sincere how it happened, and he told me that someone had made the mistake of telling Mel and Jack that he kept cash in the house. Sincere wasn't absolutely positive who ran his mouth, but he was pretty sure that it was Gary. Gary was a kid from the neighborhood who had a habit of saying more than he was supposed to around the wrong people. Sincere had been hanging with Gary the day before everything went down—and that Mel was Gary's sister's baby's father. "I don't believe in no coincidence," he said. He only believed in things he could see. And he saw Mel and Jack even though they had worn masks. The robbers kidnapped his grandfather and shot the old man, just to let Sincere know that they were serious. They wanted money, and they were ready to put holes in people to prove it.

The story woke me up to what the game was really about. Up until that point, I had believed in some sort of honor among thieves. But that illusion left my mind that night. It was all about money, and everyone was out for himself.

"I don't understand that shit, Boo-Boo, man," Sincere said. His eyes were shifting as if he expected Mel and Jack to come back at any minute. "It's like you can't even run a little business anymore," he said. "You gotta be careful around Gary."

Sincere said the same thing went down with Brian after he had hung out with Gary for a while. It wasn't that Gary was out to start any trouble. He was just excited about how well the people around him were doing. Maybe he thought that letting people know he was rubbing shoulders with important people would make him important by association. But guys like Mel and Jack always had their own plans. They came around to Brian's house to rob him. When Brian's mom refused to open the door, they tried to push their way in and wound up shooting Brian's mom in the head. I knew that Brian's mom had been shot, but I didn't know the details until that night. Sincere said that with characters like Mel and Jack running around, it was better to stay quiet about what you were getting and how much of *it* you were keeping around the house. I agreed.

It felt like Sincere was preparing me for something, but I wasn't sure what it was.

"Listen, if I give you a pair of sneakers, they're just gonna get dirty and I'ma have to buy you a new pair all over again, man," Sincere said. Then he pulled out a small wrapped bag of cocaine and told me that it contained a little bit over a gram of powder. He measured out the bag into five equal parts and wrapped them in foil. "There's five Alberts, man," he said. "Sell those to your uncles and bring me back a hundred dollars."

I had the small balls in my hand, looking at what would become my first profitable drug transaction. Sincere told me that powdered cocaine was on its way out. Everyone was moving on to selling and smoking little cooked rocks; the pieces provided the quick high of freebase cocaine. Up until then, mostly white people were freebasing, burning coke in spoons or pieces of foil. They cooked it with bleach, ammonia, or some other shit that you clean the house with that stinks. But that could fry a motherfucker's face. That's how Richard Pryor burned himself up, man. The new cooked rocks Sincere was talking about didn't involve dealing with flammable household cleaners or anything like that. He said that the profit margin wasn't as much as selling straight powder and that you couldn't get over with cutting the coke with lactose and Ajax and all that shit to stretch it out, but you could make up for it with volume because motherfuckers loved it. Users would be coming back in fifteen minutes like they ain't just smoked. Sincere said he was selling it mostly to white people coming in from Long Island, but the black folk were starting to get in on it, too. The blacks would mix it in with their weed and smoke it, and they loved the buzz. He said it started out in the Bahamas, then it spread to Miami, then it was coming from L.A., man. It was all over the place: Chicago, Detroit, San Diego, Minnesota, Boston, San Fransisco. "I could keep goin' on, but I'd just be readin' you a U.S. map," Sincere laughed. "I'm thinking these motherfuckers over here is slow to catch on, man." He was like a scholar, explaining that there had been so much cocaine in the Bahamas that they took to making it into freebase to get rid of it quicker. They were soaking it in kerosene and acid and mixing it with limestone. "But niggas ain't got time for all that shit," he said. "Niggas cut it with baking soda, then they cook that shit. Can you believe that shit, man? Baking soda? The same shit they clean the house and keep the fridge fresh with. Motherfuckin' baking soda!"

He was explaining the future to me, his mind going all over the place, from the Bahamas, to L.A., to all points on the map to the baking soda in the fridge, to the money he was going to make, to cooking the cocaine, to the little vials they would sell it in, to the pipes, bottles, and lightbulbs it was smoked in. "That shit look like little pieces of soap," he said. "Niggas smoke it in glass tubes with Brillo pads for filters." I was listening, but I really had no idea what he was talking about. I could tell that he was excited, but all the Chef Boyardee shit wasn't me. And I was still stuck on the pieces in my palm. I knew I wanted to get *it,* but I didn't see how I could work for him. I was too young. I was still in school. I didn't know the game. Sincere cocked his head back and laughed, "The only time you can't hustle is when you're six."

Once he told me that, all the doubt left me. Sincere sounded like he was speaking from experience—if he hadn't been hustling at six, he must have run into enough six-year-old hustlers to know what he was talking about. Besides, I didn't need that much convincing. I wanted to get *it* for myself and I literally had my future in my hands.

I stashed the Fat Alberts in my room. Whenever my uncles sent me out for coke, I'd just dip into my stash, walk around the block to kill some time, and then come back. When I was done with the stash, I'd go back to Sincere to re-up. I was only eleven. I was still in public school, so the only time I could hustle was after school hours, when my grandparents thought I was just playing games in the street. I picked it all up quick, because you can learn everything you need to know to hustle in under a year. The majority of things that you need to watch out for you'll see early, because everything happens so frequently. It's just the same cycle over and over. It's nothing new. You know not to say anything about what you're doing and you know it's not cool to tell on anybody. Everything else is on-the-job training.

The more I did it, the easier it got. And the easier it got, the more of *it* I got. At first, I was able to do small things like buy snacks and fast food. Then I was able to get sneakers and clothes. Then I started getting little handheld video games, but that didn't make sense: I didn't have time to play any games; I was too busy selling coke.

//////,,,,,,,//////

Crack hit the streets harder than Sincere could have imagined and I was still getting my footing when the game changed. On February 26, 1988, a rookie cop was shot dead while sitting in his patrol car in my neighborhood. He was serving guard for a witness who had agreed to testify in court against some dealers who were selling crack across the street from his house. The cop was shot five times in the head. The police said that a jailed dealer from Southside ordered the hit.

It wasn't even hours after the cop's death before the power changed hands in Southside. A few months before, the neighborhood had become the occupied territory of dealers. They were conducting business in open-air markets like they had amnesty. Half-dead, totally zoned fiends were roaming the streets day and night like the survivors of a nuclear blast. Regular people were too scared to say anything, and the cops didn't care. But when one of their own got hit, the NYPD came down hard. The streets were quickly strangled by the law's long arm and its angry fist. Outposts sprouted overnight like weeds, and patrol cars rolled through the deserted streets like tumbleweed. Battering rams sounded, sweeps were conducted, and for a minute—only for a minute—Southside looked like what it would have looked like if no one had invented crack. But it was a shock-and-awe campaign without the follow-through of a proper occupation plan. It wasn't part of a process and it wasn't a genuine change in approach. It wouldn't, couldn't last because it didn't deal with what was really going on in the community. Dealers were dealing because we needed money. The fiends needed drugs. And without jobs or viable options, that was how it was going to stay.

The rookie's murder was front-page news all over the nation and kicked the War on Drugs into high gear. Mandatory minimum drug sentences and federal sentencing guidelines had already been established in the years before, but then came the Anti-Drug Abuse Act of 1988, which called for a federal death penalty for "drug kingpins" and ensured that convicted drug offenders would serve at least 85 percent of their jail sentences. This also led to the creation of police units like the Tactical Narcotics Team (TNT) and the Street Narcotics Enforcement Unit, which gave the police an unprecedented amount of power to deal with street hustlers.

But no jobs. Without jobs, all the crackdown did was to help create a more resourceful, resilient breed of drug dealer. If the 'hood was cocaine, then the rookie cop's murder was the baking soda. And an angry police force was the fire that cooked up new hustlers. Hustlers like me.

"You gotta play for tomorrow,
even if tomorrow never comes . . ."

It wasn't safe for dealers to keep the drugs on them anymore. Not that that was ever a smart thing to do, but there was this little thing known as the United States Constitution that protected them from illegal searches. The smart thing was to keep the drugs in a stash somewhere close, probably in a brown paper bag on the floor, where it could blend in with the littered trash. Another good option was in the groove of a security gate's railing. After all, possession meant *possession* and, at the risk of sounding redundant, that meant a dealer had to actually possess the drugs, not be in proximity to them. The more creative dealers would keep their stash in the guts of a broken pay phone, behind a utility box, inside a bottomless soda can, or anything big enough to hold a sack of crack but small enough to pass detection. The hustler making enough in sales to hire help would set up with three people: one to make the sale, one to hold the product, one to serve as a lookout. But the TNT changed all that. When they swept in, everyone in the vicinity got arrested, even innocent bystanders. Just coming out of the store after purchasing a pack of sunflower seeds? *Tell it to the judge, buddy.* Running an errand for your mom? Tell it to the judge.

The TNT's tactics reversed the dealer's logic. As police squads began to stake out street-level hustlers and make arrests based on observations of sales, it made more sense to store product near one's family jewels or anywhere else the sun doesn't shine. In the event that a dealer had to run, at least he would be running with his inventory on him.

It wasn't long before it was figured out that TNT, in addition to Tactical Narcotics Team, also stood for "Tuesdays 'n' Thursdays." Those were the days the cops were most likely to roll up, hop out, and lockdown on the strip. If a hustler could outrun the cops, he was lucky. If he couldn't, well, *tell it to the judge, buddy.* The direct sale now meant that someone had part in the transaction and he could be taken down as an accessory for simply having knowledge of the sale. If you were stupid enough to be out there on a Tuesday or a Thursday, when everyone knew those black vans would roll up, and he wasn't fleet-footed enough to make it through an alley, over a wall, and through a handful of backyards to reemerge two or three blocks away, you'd be taking off your belt and shoelaces in Central Booking, eating soggy cheese sandwiches, and waiting with the rest of the slowpokes to see the judge.

A lot of this didn't apply to me at the time, though. I was too young to mark a blip on the police sonar. Because I was still too much of a small fish to compete with the full-grown sharks swimming on the boulevard, I set up shop the next block over from the best part of the strip. I had a little clientele and I was only working for about three hours after school each day. At this point, I hadn't yet graduated to making my own product or even purchasing it wholesale. I was still working on consignment. Sincere would give me half a G-pack—five hundred dollars' worth of crack, or fifty vials as opposed to a hundred—and it would take me about a week to get rid of it. Every day when I was done pumping, I'd go home and stash my money and rocks in a shoebox in the closet. I didn't tell anyone at home about my after-school business.

One day, I was at my spot down the block from the strip. I had just finished serving this fiend named Rhonda and was snuggling the last bit of my crack sack next to my nuts when Brian pulled up in a Nissan Maxima. The ride was tricked-out—spoilers, shiny spokes, dark tints—and he was rocking some truck jewelry—a thick rope chain with a large gold pendant, nugget rings on his fingers. I noticed that he was spending his money more like the kids his age, not like me—I was still just able to get some food, sneakers, a bit of clothes and maybe a video game or Walkman here and there.

Brian asked me what I was doing, and I told him that I was just hanging out. I really didn't have much to say to him. I never forgot how he played me out the year before when I asked him for sneakers. I was still pissed. He told me to hop in, and we rode without saying anything to each other for blocks before he reached over to his Kenwood stereo and lowered the volume. It rested in the dash in a Bensi pullout box, the type of stereo you could take with you when you left the ride. The lights on the sound meter bounced, like, in three colors. Boogie Down Productions' "Pussy Is Free" was playing. That song was a dealer's anthem: "The pussy is free / 'Cause the crack costs money."

"So you ain't doing nothin', eh?" he asked.

"I ain't doin' nothing," I said. "Just riding with you."

"Word?"

"Word. I'm just riding with you."

The hustler's anthem ended and Slick Rick's "Treat Her Like a Prostitute" began to play. There was no talking between songs. I realized that Brian had either bought the music or had a tape put together for him. Either way, he hadn't recorded it off the radio, which meant something. Being able to afford to do little things like buy music was a high level of the game.

Anyone who stands on the corner stands there in the entrepreneurial spirit because they really don't want to be working for anyone. The ultimate goal is to work for yourself, but the first is to look good. They see the fly shit to wear and they splurge on that so they'll feel better about how bad shit is in the 'hood. The clothes not only make the man, but they help him to escape. A dealer may have to ride the same pissy elevator as everyone else to get home, but he'll feel a bit above it if he has on new clothes or some jewelry. After he gets his wardrobe right, a dealer then graduates to buying cars, because wheels symbolize success in the 'hood. He may have the biggest house, but he can't ride around in the house for everyone to see, so a car is more important than a home in that value system. People treat the guy who looks like he has money differently. So personal-pleasure items don't really come into play until all the basics are covered. Here was Brian buying little things like music when I was still hustling for sneaker money. I had on a leather bomber over a new Adidas tracksuit with matching sneakers. On the street, I felt like I was making moves. But sitting in that car, I felt like I was hustling backward.

"Grandma got a new job?" he asked.

"A new job? Nah, she ain't got no new job."

"So Grandma musta gotta raise."

"She ain't got no raise, man. What the fuck are you talkin' about?"

"I'm talkin' about you wearing over two hundred dollars' worth of clothes on your back and seein' Rhonda walk away from you. Last time I checked, she ain't do nothin' but smoke crack."

I didn't say a thing. I couldn't believe that this nigga had the nerve to talk to *me* about what I was or wasn't doing.

"And last time I checked," he continued, "Grandma ain't had no money to spend two hundred dollars on clothes for her first grandson to stand on the street doing nothin'."

"So?"

"So I know you hustlin'."

"So?"

"So if you're just out here hustlin' for clothes, you're gonna lose the game," he said. "You can't play the game for today; you gotta play for tomorrow, even if tomorrow never comes. For every dollar you spend, you gotta save four. That's the only way you're gonna make money. I see you little guys: As soon as you get a penny, you're spending a nickel. Save your money and do somethin' with it."

I was too new to understand what he was saying. All I could remember was that he had a small sneaker store in his bedroom when we last hooked up. And now, as soon as I was able to get a little money, he's telling me not to spend it. I don't know if I was more pissed that he was flaunting his money in my face or that he was telling me what to do with mine. Years later, I realized that Brian wasn't stingy—he was just a businessman. For him, it was about business, nothing personal. He was trying to turn me onto the business side of things, but I couldn't see it then.

I told him, "I'll think about tomorrow tomorrow. But for today, I only got like an hour left out here and I'm not making any money by sitting here with you." Then he pulled over the car and I walked back to the strip. The most important thing I got out of that conversation was that I had a long way to go before I was making any real money. That's when I started to grind really hard.

"I don't gotta go to church to talk to God or to read the Bible . . ."

One Sunday morning, my grandmother woke me up to go to church. I had been out the whole day before and as late as I could stay out that night, pumping crack. I had made about eighty dollars for my pocket, which was the most I had ever made in one day. I was as tired as I could be.

"Come on, Boo-Boo," my grandmother said. "You gotta get dressed."

"I'm comin', I'm comin'," I said, but I was back asleep before she was out the door. A few minutes later, she came back and shook me awake. I didn't even get up from the bed. I just shrugged her off with my shoulder and said, "I don't wanna go."

She thought something was wrong with me. "What? Are you sick?" she asked. "Do you feel okay? Do you have a stomachache? What did you eat yesterday? You were outside all day and probably just ate something bad. Too much junk food. I'll give you some ginger ale."

"I'm okay," I said. "I just don't want to go to church."

She looked at me like I had lost my mind. "Stop talking crazy and get dressed," she said. Then she left the room and I went back to sleep. I didn't really go all the way back to sleep because I knew the conversation wasn't finished. Sure enough, after a few minutes, my grandmother came back in the room and yanked the covers off me. The shock of cold air woke me up real quick. I told her I wasn't going to church.

"What do you mean you don't want to go to church today?" she asked.

"I didn't say 'today.' I said I don't want to go to church. Star doesn't go to church. Harold doesn't go to church. Karen doesn't go—"

"Don't tell me who doesn't go to church! I go to church; I know who's not there!" I was scared. My grandmother never raised her voice, and here she was close to screaming. I knew that church was a big part of her life. She would spend all day Saturday baking cakes that she would sell to help the church raise money for renovation and maintenance. I didn't know how to explain to her that I didn't want to spend hours praising the Lord when I could be out selling drugs. It didn't make sense for me to praise the Lord in the pews only to turn around and sell crack on the highways and in the hedges. But that was a whole different conversation that I wasn't ready to have. Luckily, my grandfather came in.

"What the hell is goin' on in here?" he asked.

"Don't talk that way on the Lord's day, Curtis," my grandmother said.

All of a sudden, I wasn't so happy that my grandfather had come in. He had just gotten scolded by his wife and it was my fault. My grandfather's fists were clutched at his side like he was about to brawl. I was done for. "What's happenin'?" he asked.

"Boo-Boo said he's not going to church anymore."

"Hell," my grandfather said. "The boy don't wanna go to church, he don't gotta go to no church." My grandmother was quiet. I was saved. My grandparents had been on opposite sides of the church argument for some time. But it wasn't always like that. My grandfather used to go to mass faithfully when they attended a different church. He was so much a part of the congregation there that he had spent years as a deacon. Once he raised a couple thousand dollars for a benefit to help the church purchase a new organ. There was to be this big concert at the church, and he sold tickets and organized the band and everything. But on the night of the concert, the pastor disappeared with all the proceeds. My grandfather had to get up on the stage and apologize to the hundreds of people who had come out. After that, my grandmother switched churches, but my grandfather wouldn't step foot into another church unless a wedding or a funeral was involved.

In my room that morning, he said the same thing he had been saying for years: "Shit, I don't gotta go to church to talk to God or to read the Bible." Then he walked out of the room. My grandmother left behind him. That was the last time I went to church.

"It wasn't the drug game—
it was the drug business . . ."

Before he got locked up, my Uncle Trevor had introduced Sincere to some well-dressed Colombian fellows, one of whom was named Carlos. Like Trevor, Carlos was a class act. In the summer, he wore tailored silk and linen outfits; in the winter, expensive knit sweaters and buttery leather trench coats. Trevor and Carlos used to meet at my grandmother's house while she was at work. I think Trevor picked my grandmother's house because he was around enough to know it was safe but not around enough for anyone to track him. I remember that Carlos would always drink water, and water only. Just water. No ice. No matter how hot it was. I'd always bring him the water as an excuse to hang around and learn about the business. Whenever Trevor and Carlos were involved, it wasn't the drug game—it was the drug *business*. They were that serious about it. I learned that much and not much else because they never talked about drugs. They only talked about World Cup soccer. It would be a while before I would realize that *soccer* was a code they used to negotiate deals. All I could tell at the time was that Uncle Trevor and Carlos were very interested in the fates of the Jamaican and Mexican teams and that Carlos didn't like ice in his water.

After Trevor was sent to jail, Sincere began dealing with Carlos and became a big soccer fan. I was like, Yo, what the fuck is it with soccer? I tried to watch the game once or twice, but it wasn't in English and it came on one of those TV channels that had snowy reception. I didn't get it. When I asked Sincere what he liked so much about soccer, all he would tell me was that they call it "soccer" in the U.S. but the rest of the world refers to it as *fútbol,* and what we know as football, the rest of world knows as "American football." I told him that I didn't see what was so interesting about that. He said, "The world is a lot bigger than we know."

CHAPTER 9

I noticed that the more Sincere spoke to Carlos, the more excited he got about soccer. The more excited he got about soccer, the more money he made. The more money he made, the more money I made, so I became a soccer fan, too. I must've been the biggest soccer fan that never saw a game. Whatever team we were rooting for went on such a winning streak that I began to cop raw cocaine from Sincere. I started off with eight balls, which are one-eighth of an ounce, or three and a half grams. Then I moved up to sevens, or quarter ounces, then to half ounces. As pure cocaine it wasn't that much, but I cooked it into crack myself and came up with more vials than I ever was able to get on consignment from Sincere before he got into soccer. I was in business.

As a businessman, I had expenses. I had to go to the bodega to purchase capsules and Gem Blue Star razor blades to cut the rocks. I needed someplace to cook my product, so I wound up renting Brian's kitchen. Although Brian never gave me anything, he was the one who taught me how to cook product. He showed me the proper ratio for the batter: two parts cocaine to one part baking soda. More important, he showed me how to take the runoff from the bottom of the pot and whip it into more crack. When I did that, it was like I was doubling my supply. I couldn't believe it. By my second time at the stove, I could create a perfect mixture by eye—no measuring, no nothing. I was like, It can't be this fuckin' easy.

The only problem was the smell. I hated it at first, but I got used to it real fast. I've never forgotten that smell, either. The same way a weed smoker is tuned to the smell of burning marijuana, even if it's down the block or behind a closed door, to this day I can smell crack being cooked as soon as the water starts to boil. It's one of those weird, distinctive smells, like cigarettes, and you treat it pretty much the same way. If you smoke cigarettes, then you don't mind the smell. But when you're not smoking, even if you're a smoker, the smell gets on your nerves. With crack, I used to get bothered by the smell when I wasn't cooking it because it meant that someone was about to get money, and that someone wasn't me.

There's a rhythm to making crack. And with each step, my heart beat faster because all I really wanted to do was sell it. I'd whip up the mix, boil the water, cook it up, let it rock, piece out the rocks, stuff the vials, and hit the block.

I served any and everyone. And despite Brian's advice, I threw my profits on my back and feet. I would sneak the clothes past his grandmother but kept my extra sneakers at my friend Ray-Ray's house. He was a kid I grew up with who lived around the corner from me. He was also my first worker. When he began hustling, Ray-Ray also spent his money on sneakers, and I stashed them at my grandmother's house. Because he wore a size nine and I wore a seven, my grandmother never caught on that I had extra money. Once in a while, she would ask why Ray-Ray wouldn't just take his sneakers home.

"I know," I'd say, acting like I was annoyed at Ray-Ray. "I keep telling him to come get them. I'm just gonna toss them in a bag. I don't care."

/////,,,,,,,/////

As all good things must, Sincere's winning streak came to an end. The problem was that Sincere was of the opinion that everyone who bet on the soccer games should ride out the loss with him—he jacked up his prices on me. Like that wasn't bad enough, he also decided to shortchange Carlos. That's how I learned how to play *fútbol*.

Despite Sincere's moves, Carlos wanted to continue business with him. Sincere had all the right connections in the 'hood, and the profit was too large for Carlos to ignore. "I make good business with Sincere," Carlos said. "But he doesn't realize that sometimes you win and sometimes you lose. And when you lose, you shouldn't take everyone down with you. It's just not the way men work."

If I had had the clientele, Sincere would have been cut out of the picture. As it was, Carlos began to deal with me directly. He told me that he remembered that I always got him water when he met with my Uncle Trevor. He said that he could only trust a man who was willing to serve another man. Then he gave me my first kilogram of cocaine. It was tightly packed in plastic wrap and looked like a solid brick of powdered sugar.

I took the brick to Brian's house and used his triple-beam balance to divide it up into eighths, half ounces, and quarter ounces. I kept half of the brick to cook into pieces and sold the rest of the weight to other dealers. I was still in junior high school and I was supplying guys who were twice my age. It was about this time that school became a joke. I knew all the math I needed to know after I divided my first brick. When my guidance counselor encouraged me to get working papers, I nearly laughed in his face. Working papers were the fast-food card. If I filled out a bunch of paperwork, I would get a nice little card that would allow me to get a job at a fast-food spot. If I had been really lucky, I'd be able to work the register and not be stuck in the back. Nothing I was being told in school made sense to my reality; even less seemed to be able to get me out of that reality. The only thing that mattered to me was making money, because money seemed to be the answer to all my problems.

Being higher on the supply end of the drug equation didn't bring as much profit, but it took less work and it bolstered my status in the neighborhood. After I sold off my second kilo, I quickly invested in a third, which I divided by grams. I stashed a quarter kilo for storage and bagged up two eighths. If someone could have taken one of the eighths off my hands, my stock in the 'hood would have skyrocketed. A fourteen-year-old kid selling eighths? I would've been a child prodigy. I paid fifty dollars for a beeper the size of a deck of cards and began moving as much of the raw coke as I could. The other half of the brick had been broken down into eight balls, sevens, and fourteens. I moved them easy, even though I had to keep the beeper under my pillow so my grandmother wouldn't hear it.

One time, Chance kept beeping me, but I couldn't get back to him because my grandmother was on the phone. Chance was this guy I had sold a couple of sevens to. I had to go to a pay phone to call him back because I was worried about losing the sale. There's no brand loyalty in the drug game. It's like a trickle-up policy: The fiends will cop from whoever's around or whoever will give them the best deal. If you let a fiend get over with a short—like giving him a dime for nine dollars—he'll come back to you, not because he's loyal but because he's looking for a bargain. If someone else lets him get over with shorts, he's gonna forget about you before he lights his pipe. That's what it is, demand and supply. I think it's taught backward in school. There, it's "supply and demand," where companies come up with a whole bunch of shit and supply it. Then the companies fool people into thinking that they need the shit they're pushing, thereby creating an artificial demand. But the streets figured it correctly: The demand comes first, and whoever has the supply will profit.

In many ways, the dealers are as addicted as the fiends. We count on them for our livelihood. It's like politicians. Most politicians don't have any respect for the people who vote for them and they feel like they're above their voters. But come election time, they're at the voters' mercy.

When I finally got in touch with Chance, he was asking me a whole bunch of questions about why I took so long to call him back. I told him my grandmother was on the phone, but he sounded like he didn't believe me. He kept asking me questions until I was like, "Do you want the coke or not?" He told me he'd be right there.

When Chance pulled up to the park where I was waiting, I could tell he was mad. He had some guy I had never seen before, sitting in the car and staring at me real hard. Chance kept looking around and asked me what took me so long to call him back. I thought he was going to try to rob me, so I reached under my shirt like I had a gun at my waist. I would never do anything like that today, because if someone thinks I have a gun and I really don't, then he may wind up shooting me when he didn't even intend to. A scared person will shoot you twice as fast as an angry one. But I was young and stupid.

"You keep asking me a lot of questions, homeboy," I said. I was holding the gun that wasn't there in my hand and motioning like I was going to pull it out any second.

I saw the guy in the car's eyes go wide. Chance backed up and said, "That last bag was light, homeboy."

Shit. He *was* trying to rob me. "Light?" I asked. "What the fuck do you mean 'light'?"

"I bought a quarter ounce from you," he said. "It was supposed to be seven grams, but it was only six."

"Get the fuck outta here," I said. If I really had had a gun, then I probably would have shot him right there. I was being tested, and the way I maneuvered the situation was going to set a precedent. If I let Chance get over on me, then that's who I would be in the streets: that nigga you can get over on. I had to rearrange the discussion to where I was in a position of power, and I had to do it fast.

"I sold off damn near four whole bricks and nobody said nothin'," I lied. "You tryin' to play me, homeboy? I come all the way out here to break you off from my last ounce—from my private stash—and this is how you try to play me?" I looked over Chance's shoulder to the guy in the car and met his eyes. When he looked away, I acted like I was raising the gun from my waist. "Man, I oughta—"

Chance threw his hands up over his face. "Chill, homeboy," he said, looking at the ground. "I'm just saying the bag was light."

"Fuck you and your light bag," I said and walked away. When I got to the corner, I looked over my back and saw Chance arguing with the guy in the car. I turned the corner and ran all the way home.

That night, I kept having nightmares that I was being chased. Everyone was there. Carlos, Sincere, Brian, Chance, Rhonda—everyone I had been dealing with on the street. And everyone was trying to rob me and kill me. In one dream, Carlos looked disappointed and kept talking about trust. "How can we do business as men when I cannot trust you?" Carlos asked. He kept asking me why I wasn't returning his beeps. I said that I hadn't gotten any beeps from him and showed him my beeper. I tried to scroll through the numbers, but it was broken and only Chance's number showed up. I told Carlos that my beeper was broken and that's probably why I didn't return the calls. I never got them. Then he asked me why I had pulled a gun on him.

"Gun?" I asked. "I never pulled a gun on you!" I yelled at Carlos.

Carlos was looking down, and his hands were in front of his face. "This is not how men do business, Boo-Boo," he said. I looked at my hands. I was pointing the beeper at him. Only it wasn't a beeper—it was a gun. I had never held a real gun at that point, and I had no idea how it got there. Carlos was in front of me, frozen, talking about how men do and do not do business. Pulling guns on each other was *not* how men did business, he pointed out. "I thought you were a man of respect, Boo-Boo," he said. "I see I was wrong. You disappoint me."

When Carlos said that, I remember thinking, Oh fuck. Now I have to shoot him. I went to pull the trigger, but then the gun in my hand started to beep. *Beep! Beep! Beep!*

Beep!

Beep!
Beep!

Then I woke up, and my heart was thumping out of my chest. My beeper was going off underneath the pillow, but I was halfway off the bed. I crawled to the beeper and saw that it was Chance calling. When I called him back the next day, he wanted to know if I still had any of my "private stash" left that I could sell him.

///////..........//////

Even though I passed my first real test in the street game, I knew there were more to come. I just didn't realize how soon they would come or how close to home they would hit. It was beginning to dawn on me how dangerous the game I was playing was. At no point, though, did I look at things as a sign that I was supposed to do something other than sell drugs. All I realized was that I had to be more careful. I would continue to sell drugs because it was the only thing that I knew and the only thing that seemed to make sense. I couldn't understand the idea of going to school for another six years or more to make less money than I could make in six months. I viewed the potential violence as part of the price I had to pay to get what I wanted. Had I chosen to go to school, I would have had to deal with homework and people telling me what to do. And even then, I most likely would have wound up behind the dealers I saw in my neighborhood. It was a simple choice, really.

I figured I'd simply have to fortify my hustling defenses, but I didn't get the chance right then because in the next couple of days, more people began to complain that my bags were light. I was like, What the fuck? I thought that scaring off Chance would have been enough to keep me safe, but it wasn't.

I went by Brian's house to tell him what was going on. "Niggas is just trying you cuz you young," he said. "If you take it like a pussy, niggas is always gonna try to fuck you." He took out the same triple-beam scale that we used to weigh my cuts and placed some packages he had bagged on it. All of them were copacetic. "Nobody ever came at me with that dumb 'light' shit," he said. "But then again, I ain't no little nigga new to the game."

That was it for me. I got it in my head that niggas were trying to play me. I decided that I was going to cop a gun from Old Man Dan as soon as I knocked off the rest of the brick.

When I got home, I caught Uncle Star coming out of my room. It seemed weird because he never checked for me, especially not enough to go into my room to look for me. But I wasn't even thinking about that. I was going to take one-eighth of the kilo and run back to Brian's house to cook it up. I was gonna put the whole middle-management aspect of my business on the back burner until I could afford some security. When I checked my closet, I saw that the lid of the sneaker box where I kept the bagged-up product wasn't secure. That fucked with me because I always made sure I kept it hidden underneath a bunch of coloring books and toys I'd had since I was a kid. I had to move a trunk filled with green army men, broken robots, and remote-control cars every time I wanted to get to the stash. But the trunk was pushed off to the side and the sneaker box wasn't properly closed. Suddenly everything made sense.

Small things had been going missing around the house for some time. My grandfather had been saying that his wallet kept coming up twenty dollars short and he could not recall where he spent the money. He said that either he was going senile in his old age or Bush had raised taxes overnight. My grandmother was a bit more suspicious. She had approached me about taking money from her dresser. I wanted to say, "I got ten pairs of sneakers and more clothes than I can hide from you at Ray-Ray's house," but I couldn't say that. She knew something was going on with me, so she began to keep a closer eye on me, screening my phone calls and asking more questions. She even started locking her bedroom door. I'll never forget the way she looked at me the moment she stopped trusting me. It hurt me to know that she thought I was a thief, almost enough for me to tell her what I was doing. But I didn't. I didn't have any answers for her.

Looking at my trunk pushed to the side and the shoe-box lid out of place, I had all the answers I needed. I knew that Star was now using drugs more than anyone else in the house. I knew he had reached the point where he couldn't have a good time without getting high on the weekends. But I had no idea he had actually become an addict to the point where he'd steal in the house. I went into the living room, where Star was watching television. I asked him what he was doing in my room. He said, "I was looking for a pen. I needed to write something down."

I was like, What? I had never seen this motherfucker write down a thing in my life. I stepped between him and the television. "What did you have to write down? I don't see you writing nothing." I really needed to hear him say it. I wanted him to confess to stealing. Even if no one was there to hear it, even if it wouldn't erase the way my grandmother had kept me at a distance, I needed to hear him say it.

He got up and pushed me across the room. Before I knew it, I was lying on the floor with broken china at my elbows. I decided that I didn't need to hear him say what he had been up to. I just wanted to kill him. I jumped up and grabbed the large wooden fork that was hanging on the wall and began hitting him with it.

Whap! I was really trying to kill this nigga. *Whap!* He had everyone in the house looking at me like I was a thief. *Whap!* Motherfuckers on the street could have killed me. *Whap!* He didn't have to confess. *Whap!* I'd be just as happy killing him. *Whap!* He was so fucked up, he couldn't even fight back. On the last blow, the fork split down the middle. *Whrack!*

Cynthia came running into the room to break up the fight. I ran upstairs, grabbed my shoe box, and left the house. When I reweighed everything at Brian's house, I saw that this nigga Star was on some real crackhead shit. He had opened up each bag, took out a little bit, and closed it back up. He must have pinched about a hundred grams of cocaine out of the kilo. There was also a whole quarter-ounce bag missing. I would have been pissed, but I was too busy being scared shitless. I was in something I wasn't sure I could get out of. If the guys I had been selling light bags to thought that I was cheating them on purpose, they would have killed me. I didn't even want to think about what would happen if Carlos thought I was playing with his money. As it was, I had only less than an eighth of the kilo in my possession, and that wasn't even enough to pay my tab with Carlos. Even if I sold off everything, I'd still be close to a thousand dollars short on his consignment payment. Having spent all my money on sneakers and tracksuits didn't help.

I decided to sell off most of the powder in order to get my good name back. If I didn't get back on proper standing with the people I was working with, not only would I not be able to make any money, but my life wouldn't be worth shit on the strip. At first, I was going to overstuff the bags, but then Brian told me that would be the same as admitting I was wrong, and being wrong was being weak. "You might as well give it away for free if you're gonna do that," he said. "Because niggas will come and take you if you show weakness." So I sold off the raw at normal weight and kept three and half grams for myself. I cooked up the three and a half grams, pieced it out into vials, and sold it hand to hand. When I was done, I flipped that money and copped seven grams from Brian. I cooked that up and sold it off in two days. Then I copped a half ounce, which I then flipped into one hundred and twenty-five grams in another six days. I was on the strip the whole time. At no point did I go home.

Brian told my grandmother that he was watching me after the fight with Star, and she left it at that. It was summertime, and I took power naps on a bench or in the grass when I got tired. I only came off the strip to go to Brian's to cop and cook. I didn't even let the crack cookies dry. I sliced them into pieces while they were still soft as wet soap. I was desperate. My skin was thick with sweat and dirt to the point where I felt trapped in myself. I smelled so bad that I burned my nose every time I took a whiff of myself. I was too focused to realize that I wasn't centered. I was so busy looking at my escape I didn't see that for a short period of time, there was very little difference between me and the fiends I was serving. But within two weeks, I had all the money I owed Carlos and then some. The only reason I could go that hard was because I knew I had to get that money back.

That was a major lesson for me. From there I learned that you can't trust anyone in the drug business, not even your family. To this day, Star and I don't speak much behind his pinching my inventory. He may not have realized it at the time, but he was practically setting me up to be killed. How do you forgive that? What do you say? *You almost got me killed, but that's in the past? I understand why it happened, and I forgive you?*

Nah. It doesn't go away that easy.

*"My ability to control
my anger during confrontation
was my edge . . ."*

After all the drama with Star and Chance, I started boxing. There was an older dealer named Freedom, from the Biasley projects, who opened up a small gym on the strip. Freedom reminded me of my Uncle Trevor— he was a bad guy, but he was a *good* bad guy. He had a Toyota 4Runner with a customized Gucci interior and a set of Jet Skis hitched to the back. But he also put his money into a gym so that kids in the 'hood would have some place to go other than the corner.

Kids will pick up on things early. They're going to want to do whatever they saw on TV. If there's gymnastics on in the house, the kid's going to want to do gymnastics. If you have *Superman* on all day, that kid's going to want to fly. If a kid watches a show with a lot of fighting and flipping, that kid's going to be running around the house doing all that shit. Then their mom will put them in karate school or something like that because the kid got the idea from watching TV.

When that kid goes into karate school, he's going to learn more than just how to punch and kick and all that. That's what he went into it for—the physical benefits. He got into it because he wanted to do what he saw on television, but it's not that easy. He has to work hard at it. He has to do the "wax-on/wax-off" thing for a while, doing the same thing over and over again. But if he sticks with it, that instills discipline in him. That's what boxing did for me. It stopped me from getting angry when I fought.

I was big for my age, over one hundred and fifty pounds at fourteen years old when I began boxing. Matches were determined by weight, not age, and there were no fourteen-year-old boys sparring, so I regularly found myself going head-up with teens who were way older than me. In the ring, age and status didn't matter. The coolest kid on the street and the most unknown nobody who never left his house were even as long as they belonged to the same weight class. Boxing was the great equalizer. And it was the one sport that I could take part in where I had no one to blame for my success or failure other than myself. I liked that.

I won't front: At first, my opponents routinely got the best of me. I was going down like I had extra gravity on me. But then, Sammy, my coach, told me something that made no sense to the logical mind, yet it must have taken root somewhere deep inside of me because it altered my entire game. "In the ring, heart is everything," Sammy said. "But technique is more important than heart."

Once I got it in my head that the game was as much psychological as it was physical, things changed. I learned that a large part of anything physical in this world is how you think about it mentally. The reason Mike Tyson was able to beat a lot of his opponents early on was because he convinced the world that nobody could beat him. As soon as someone signed on to fight Mike Tyson, even their own mother would give up on him, like, "You're going to fight Mike? Oh. Well, maybe he won't hurt you *too* bad." So even the fighter himself was going through some shit because, out the gate, he didn't feel like he could beat Tyson. It wasn't until Tyson got beat that fighters started to come at him. Now he's having a hard time, but before, when he had everyone's heart, he was the scariest guy on two legs. So I learned to block out my opponent's shit-talking and tuck away my emotions.

I still lost. But I began to see how and why I was losing. I was like a scientist analyzing the fight from a remote location inside my head: *See, he's been jabbing with the left for a minute now. He's trying to get you off his right. He's saving up energy. Before he comes with the right, he's gonna make that funny move with his left shoulder. He always does that.*

Bam! Right in my face.

Okay, he did just like you thought. You're on the ropes now, but it's okay. You just weren't quick enough.

I analyzed my matches from the rope a lot. Sometimes I analyzed from the floor. But it was okay; I was getting better. My strategies were coming together quicker than my ability to carry them out, but I was cool with that because I knew I would become quicker through practice. Fighting every day took away the emotions that went with fighting. And I saw that the more I was able to keep my anger in check, the more I improved.

When I was in the ring, all my problems and worries reduced. My beef with Star, hiding from my grandmother, my concerns about being taken advantage of on the strip—it all became embodied in my opponent. When I boxed, I had someone in front of me and my intention was to hurt that man. But as I got knocked upside my head, I began to realize that my anger didn't stem from losing the match as much as it did from my outside problems. I learned to keep my emotions in line in the ring and to be less invested in hurting my opponent. Before I boxed, I was more likely to fight mad. I was reacting more on emotion than being conscious of my opponent's movements, and that took me off point. I realized that if I stuck with it and stayed calm enough, everything else would fall into place inside and outside the ring. I was able to deal with my problems for what they were without having my feelings take over.

The gym became my third home. When I wasn't killing time in school, I was sparring in the gym or selling crack on the strip. Soon, I was fighting any and everyone on the streets, even the guys who felt they shouldn't be fought. I had already been going up against guys who were older than me, who underestimated me and talked shit, so the normal intimidation tactics that guys use in the streets didn't phase me. When I went into a fight in the streets, it was because I chose to fight. If someone was talking shit to me, I'd just be like, "All right, let's fight." It didn't bother me to get into an altercation because I was so used to getting knocked around in the gym anyway.

I actually did better in the streets than I did in the ring. In the gym, I was going toe-to-toe with more accomplished fighters who knew what they were doing. The guys on the streets had no technique. I picked up a few tricks from my street fights, but for the most part, winning in the street just gave me confidence in the ring. That began a serious cycle, because my confidence from the street wins led to more wins in the ring. And the more I won in the ring, the more fights I picked in the streets. At the slightest infraction, I was punching someone in the face. From that first punch, if he wanted to take it higher and make it a real match, I'd let him take a swing or two. When a guy has no formal training, it doesn't take much to note his pattern and make him pay for his mistakes.

He keeps dropping his hand every time he goes for my head. The next time he goes for my head, he's gonna drop his hand and then I'ma punch the shit out of him. Once he's in a compromising situation, I'ma get regular on him. I'ma kick him in his fuckin' head, try to kill his ass out there. We in the street. It don't matter. Ain't no rules.

My technique was my sword, but my ability to control my anger during confrontation was my edge. The calmer and more confident I became, the more I fought. The more I fought, the less I got hit. The less I got hit, the more people got stomped in the head. The more people got stomped in the head, the calmer and more confident I became. After about six months, word got around that it was better to leave me be. People were like, "That little nigga may be plump, but he fast."

*"He was as mean a bastard as
the drug game ever bred . . ."*

Godfather still controlled a lot of the higher-level drug distribution in my neighborhood, and he was turning his empire into a family business. He had three sons, Derrick, Shawn, and Jermaine.

Derrick was the oldest and a big shot, mainly due to his father's influence. He was cut from the cloth of middle management—that is, he could tell you what to do fine enough and take credit for it even better. But that was about the extent of his usefulness. His sole status was his proximity to Godfather's ear and heart. But Godfather wasn't a fool. He trusted his Derrick to do only three types of things: the easiest, the least important, or those that were really unnecessary but could be seen to be highly important if you didn't know any better. Basically, Derrick was a glorified errand boy.

Shawn was the middle son. I'm not going to say that he was quite fond of the penal system, but I will say that he easily chalked it up to fate that he'd spent more days behind bars than underneath the sun. Going to jail did not seem to bother Shawn the least bit. In his mind, he must have lived in jail, visiting home for a few months at a time. When his brief moments at home were interrupted with an arrest and he had to head back to the rent-free life of the Big House, he'd be like, "I don't care." I think that was his favorite phrase: *I don't care.* I don't know if he said it to fool himself or to lie to the people around him. He just said it with an easy shrug of his shoulders and kept it moving. If he was going back to jail on a parole violation after only being home for six months, he'd be like, "I don't care." When he found out that the feds wouldn't let his state sentence run concurrently with his parole and he'd be shipped back to Alabama after he served three years in New York, he was like, "I don't care."

CHAPTER 8

The youngest was Jermaine, but everyone called him Red because he was light-skinned with sunburned hair. Maybe Derrick and Shawn made Godfather question whether he had the ability to produce kids who retained any bit of his spirit, but Red was his father's son in the ways that really mattered. Where Derrick was about showmanship and Shawn was indifferent, Red was enterprising and visionary. And he was as mean a bastard as the drug game ever bred. After coming home from a short stint in prison, Red locked down the strip and took full control of *everything*. And not just the strip. He also secured the crack business in Rochdale Village, a private housing complex on the east side of the boulevard. Rochdale consists of nearly six thousand apartment units and contains its own shopping complex. It's the type of score that ordinary hustlers can only dream of. But Red was no ordinary hustler.

The first thing Red did was sell purple-topped capsules, the biggest and baddest vials available. This made it hard to sell anything on the strip because once the fiends got a load of purple tops, everything else was a rip-off. The second thing he did was clear the strip of competition the old-fashioned way. This made it hard to sell anything else on the strip because, well, if you tried to sell anything that wasn't a purple top, you'd probably get shot.

Unlike most everyone else, Ray-Ray and I were warned to stop selling pieces. "Who told y'all you can hustle around here?" Red asked us. We were like, What? What do you mean, "Who told us we could hustle?" It's a free fuckin' country. We couldn't believe the nerve of this guy, coming fresh out the pen and telling us what to do like he was the president of the boulevard. We thought this nigga was crazy, like, *It didn't stop being a free country just because your dumb ass got locked up. Wasn't you just in jail this morning?* Of course we ain't saying shit. Red was a mean son of a bitch when he went in, and the chances of him mellowing out behind bars rested somewhere between none and negative less than none. We told him we were gonna move off the strip, but in our heads, we were like, We gon' hustle right here like we was doin' while your stupid ass was spending time in the mountains.

I didn't have much choice. After my run-ins with Chance and Star, I had slowed down to copping only as much raw cocaine as I knew I could move. Carlos didn't have time for penny-ante dealers, so I was back to copping eighths and hand-to-hand sales. But now Red was trying to put an end to even that. "Y'all little niggas can't hustle here no more," he said. "You wanna hustle? You gotta get packs from me. Ain't nothing movin' out here but purple tops."

I was like, No fuckin' way. There was no way I was taking packs. Buying prebottled crack was one more step backward down the food chain than I was willing to take. Of course I didn't say shit. I kept my mouth shut and I kept pushing my pieces.

A few days later, we saw Red again. When he was walking toward us, we just snickered, like, "I told you not to sell on the strip." We were making fun of him, but not in a way that he could hear. There was nothing funny about the situation, but the whole thing was really absurd. How could a guy fresh out of jail come around and tell us where we could and couldn't hustle? That made no fuckin' sense. Ray-Ray said, "Look, here he come. He gonna tell us to get off the strip." I said, "He ain't telling me shit." I was right; he didn't say a thing. He just walked over and landed a blow squarely on my chest. My shoulders closed in on each other like a book that's been slammed shut, and I went down. Hard.

By the time the black spots went away, Ray-Ray was on the floor next to me and Red was walking away, muttering that he told us to stop hustling on the strip. There were a bunch of people out there. No one said a thing. "Do you know what this means?" Ray-Ray asked me after he came off the floor and was trying to shake the sense back into his skull.

"Yeah," I said. "Next time we see him comin', we're gonna have to run."

It went like that for about a week or two—the selling, the running, the ducking, the punching, the dizziness. Each time he caught us, the beatings got a little more brutal—nothing devastating enough to cause any real trauma, just a few lumps. Even though I was boxing, there wasn't anything I could do about Red. When it came to fighting, I was scared of him; the fight was over before it started. We started treating Red like he was the police: *If he don't see us sellin' nothin', then we ain't sellin' nothin'.* But we wouldn't run, because running was like admitting guilt. We figured that we could continue to sell our pieces on the low as long as we played it cool when Red came around. This worked. Sorta.

It was so much wishful thinking. Red was just too fuckin' mean and too fuckin' smart. We didn't really start to see how smart he was until one day when we were on the strip, supposedly not hustling. Red was across the street with John-John, Ray-Ray's stepbrother. It's like he was staking out the strip, waiting to see who had the nerve to push anything but purple tops. We spent half the afternoon not selling a thing. Surely Red would see that we were playing by his rules and leave us alone. After a while, John-John strolled over and asked Ray-Ray what he was doing.

"Whu—"

Bam!

Before Ray-Ray could answer, he was floating backward through the air. Then John-John walked back across the street. We got the message loud and clear. Anybody who would lay out his own brother on the floor was not playing. I made the decision to switch to selling purple tops before Ray-Ray hit the ground. It was just too much shit. We still tried to get our pieces off on the side, but it didn't make any sense. The word was out that the big value-packed purple tops were the best high for your dollar. No self-respecting crack fiend would shortchange himself by buying anything else. A crackhead would get insulted and look at a dealer like he was trying to rob them if he offered something less than the best. They're finicky like that.

Some of the other hustlers attempted to compete and did well by pushing illusions. Illusions were vials with coned bottoms, longer caps, and thicker glass. They trick the buyers' eyes into thinking they're getting more rock than they really are. But all that ended when Junior came through with his crew from Brooklyn. Once Junior and his boys began letting their pistols talk, no one sold anything but purple tops. That's when Ray-Ray and I realized that we had gotten off lucky with a few beatdowns.

Red came up with the plan to bring in outside guns while he was serving time upstate in Elmira. Like most correctional facilities, Elmira was a place where inmates actually became better criminals. Red met Junior in the yard, and they quickly recognized each other through their street reputations. Godfather's growing legend in the cocaine game had spread through the five boroughs, and Junior's standing as a notorious stickup artist preceded him. Red figured that if he had a few guns like Junior's, he could do some big things when he got back home. Junior had only a few more months left on his sentence, and he liked to do big things. With Junior's loose pistols and Red's tight rules, the strip would be sealed shut.

A person is more liable to act right when a stranger has a gun pointed at him. If a familiar face shows up with a weapon, there's room for a conversation—"Why you pullin' out on me? I thought we was cool?"— which is actually room to get shot. If someone's fucked-up enough in the head to pull a gun on someone he knows, he's probably fucked-up enough to shoot that person. Even if he doesn't intend to shoot, all the questions could send the guy over the edge, like, "Why you askin' me all these fuckin' questions?" But when a stranger pulls out a gun on someone, it's assumed that the guy with the gun is going to shoot. As long as he's a variable in that equation, it's best to go with what it looks like: He has a gun, he will shoot.

That being said, Junior's crew wound up letting their guns go off regularly on the strip. Some of the hustlers out there refused to be robbed on their own turf. Much in the same way that it's hard to win a war when fought on enemy territory, home pride caused some excess violence on the strip. Still, it didn't take Junior long to lock things down. Most of the hustlers knew of his rep and wouldn't dare test him. When Junior came through with his crew, he made everyone who was not working for Red get up off all their cash and work. That's when all Red's days of staking out the strip started to make sense: He had been doing surveillance. He gave Junior all the info—who held the cash, where the product was stashed, who to shoot first if someone acted up. When Junior's crew rolled up, they were able to neutralize any potential conflict before it had a chance to show its head.

When something did jump off, it was taken care of quickly. Their murder game was serious, and the crew had the advantage of being able to flee back to Brooklyn while the dealers remained easy targets on the strip. It was a losing proposition for the hustlers, and after a few weeks there was nothing moving on the strip but purple tops. And once there was nothing moving on the strip but purple tops, the entire Rochdale housing complex fell into line. Purple tops were such a bargain that the addicts on the boulevard began sending referrals from the Forties houses and the Baisley projects to the strip. A few of the fiends even moved onto the strip because it made no sense for them to keep traveling back and forth all day. They jut stayed there all day selling stuff, begging for money, and getting high off those purple tops. This is the world I lived in; this was my reality.

//////''''''''''//////

Red was sitting on a bench on the Rochdale side of Guy R. Brewer Boulevard. His three cars—a Nissan Maxima, a Ford Bronco, and a Ferrari 308 GTS—were parked in front of him. When he called me over, I was scared. Red was the only one moving serious crack on our side of things, so the price of raw coke had dropped to entice competition. A few days before, me and Ray-Ray had resorted to cooking our own pieces and stuffing them inside purple-topped capsules. I figured that Red would put one and one together once word got to him that we hadn't re-upped in almost a week.

"Come 'ere, Curt." He always called me by my government name. "Y'all can't be doing that shit no more," Red said. I tried to play like I didn't know what he was talking about, but he ignored me.

"I'm not gonna go back to chasing y'all," he said, but it sounded more like, "I'm making believe I don't know what's going on because if I acknowledge that you're lying to me in my face, then I'm going to have to make a decision I really don't want to make." When he looked at me, it almost looked like he was begging. "I ain't chasing y'all little motherfuckers no more," he said. "You can run from Junior."

I knew he meant it, but that's not what made me get back under his wing. I had a stash of crack in my drawers, but it didn't make any sense to keep selling my own stuff. I had been pushing the bootleg purple tops since the top of the week and I wasn't seeing any profit, even with the discounted coke prices. Actually, when I factored in all the labor and overhead, it seemed like I was losing money. I told Red that I didn't see how he could make any money by putting so much crack in each capsule.

He explained that the game wasn't about the hard sell, it was about the fast flip. "You don't make money from fiends," he said. "You make money from moving product. The more product you move, the more money goes through your hands. The more money goes through your hands, the more money you make."

I still didn't get it. I got the part about making more money based on more money going through my hands. That part was simple. But the rest of it didn't make sense. If I couldn't make a profit on a few vials, then I didn't see how selling more nonprofit vials would make me money. I just saw it as making me a whole lot more nonprofit. My mentality was that you had to make as much money as you could, and you did that by charging as much as you could per unit.

Red told me that I was working with a flawed business model. "You have to negate the competition by offering a better product," he said. "Once you've negated the viability of the competition, you can concentrate efforts on increasing your business." He spoke like he had spent a lot of time reading in jail. It seemed like every time someone went to jail for a long time, he came back with a whole new vocabulary. And not just slang. Motherfuckers would go to jail and come back talking pro-black and breaking down racism. Or they'd come back religious, quoting chapters and verses of the Koran or the Bible. One guy I knew even came back a Buddhist. Red came back an economics major.

"There's only three modes to increase your business," he said. "First off, you can increase your number of clients. But sooner or later, you're gonna reach market saturation. The market gets tapped. It's like you can't sell pictures to a blind man. When you look around this current marketplace, all you see is market saturation. So that leaves the other two modes of increasing business: increasing the average sale per customer or increasing the amount of sales per client—you know, the number of times said client will return for a purchase. Now, it's hard to increase the sale per client because a fiend that's coming for ten is gonna come for ten, and a fiend that comes for twenty is gonna come for twenty. If you decrease the amount or quality of the product to increase your profit per sale, you're gonna lose the clientele. Fiends may be fiends, but they ain't stupid. They're bargain shoppers. A wise, entrepreneurial man such as myself has to offer the biggest and best product available, which will result in a greater bottom line in the tangible form of return customers. When I combine such a strategic approach vis-à-vis an increased revenue base for my downline—such as volume discounts and performance bonuses, et cetera and so forth—I create a workforce that is just as invested in the success of my enterprise. The more they sell, the more they make. The more they make, the more I make. It's really simple."

He looked at me like I should have gotten what he had just said, but I had no earthly idea as to what bullshit he was shoveling. But I could see his cars in front of my face. I had never seen a Ferrari in real life before that. A Ferrari was something you saw in a magazine or on TV, not in the 'hood. I knew that Red was in Elmira less than three months ago, so I knew *something* had to be going on. But when he opened his mouth, all I heard was, *I told you little motherfuckers to stop hustling. You keep pushing your own pieces and I'ma let Junior shoot you. That's all I really called you over here to say. I'm just giving you this ghetto economics lesson to fuck with your head.*

Red picked up a crumpled lunch bag that he had beside him and then slid into the cockpit of the Ferrari. He told me to get in. We drove over to Baisley projects, where selling drugs was more of a movement than a business or a game. Baisley was organized under the Pharaohs, who were members of the Nation of Kings and Queens, which was an Egyptian-based religion that a lot of guys converted to during their time in prison. In jail, being a Pharaoh was based on finding strength and safety in numbers. When the Pharaohs came home, they just applied what the religion had taught them to the streets. They asserted that they were the descendants of kings wrongfully removed from power and enslaved by the white man, who had been cast out of their land thousands of years before Christ, a black man, walked the earth. They said that America was a modern-day Babylon and that in order to make it here, they had to gain economic power. The fact that they sold crack to their own people was of no consequence, because their ends would justify their means. Much of it was mumbo jumbo and pseudoscience, but to kids who needed something, anything, to belong to, it provided many answers.

When we got close to the projects, I saw kids on top of buildings talking into big walkie-talkies. By the time we got to the courtyard on the Guy Brewer side of the projects, there was a group of Pharaohs waiting for us. The more important ones were playing a dice game, but there were about six younger guys standing around them the way Secret Service agents stand around the president.

Red disregarded the security and joined in the dice game. He took a wad of money from the brown bag and then handed me the bag. Red rolled the dice and began taking their money. At first, he was hitting them up for twenties. Then fifties. Every time Red rolled, he won. Regardless, most of the Pharaohs and their minions refused to quit. The logic of the dice says that the only money that can win is the money on the ground. Riding out a losing streak inevitably gives way to a win, sooner or later.

But after Red won a few more hands, three of the Pharaohs decided it was better to save money than to save face. They dropped out of the game, and Red handed me a fat jumble of winnings to put in the bag. That really pissed off the guys. "You need to let us win some of our money back, brother," one of them said. He was talking to Red, but he was staring at me.

"Well, you 'mighty kings' are gonna have to win something first," Red joked. "Ain't that right, Curt?"

I managed to clear my throat and squeak out a broken-voiced uh-huh. It came out a lot weaker than I had intended, but what the fuck was I gonna do? I thought that Red had lost his senses. All of his earlier talk about making more money by making less profit seemed to fit my theory: Red was insane. I couldn't understand how he could take these guys' money, take a swipe at their religion, and then ask me to cosign his madness. No way.

"Don't worry," Red said to the Pharaohs. "If you great African kings can win it back, it's yours. It's right here, man. It's okay, *my brothers,* I ain't gonna do you like the white man did. I promise."

Red was pissing into an open wound. And the Pharaohs didn't like it one bit. One of them moved around behind me. I couldn't see what he was doing, but I wasn't going to turn around to look. After my voice cracked, I couldn't trust my body not to betray me by a wince or make some other motion of fear. Another guy reached under his shirt, pretty much the same way I had that night with Chance. But I knew this one wasn't bluffing. He walked around in short jerky movements and just kept talking to no one about how he was ready to go to war with the savage who was disrespecting him in his own house. Another just walked over to a short fence, propped himself up, and stared me down while a nervous twitch ran through his leg.

Red ignored all this and shook the dice—"Daddy needs a new Ferrari!" He was picking up his winnings when I saw King Amenhotep the Magnificent walking toward the game. Amenhotep was so respected in the Nation of Kings and Queens that everyone just called him "King," the way the president of this country is "Mr. President." It was obvious who was being talked about and that was that. I was already scared, but when I saw King, I got . . . I don't know if there's a word for it. You'd have to come up with a phrase, something like *ultimately deathly terrified*. And that would only begin to explain how I felt when I saw King walking toward me.

King was, in a word, notorious. He had previously been an enforcer for the organization, but the feds had indicted the leaders of his Pharaohs a few months before. The old bosses still ran things from the pen, but King was left in charge of street operations while his bosses' lawyers scoured the law encyclopedias for appeal loopholes. King's rep was built on disappearing Colombian connections, tortured workers, and public murders. People who were set to testify against him usually changed their minds, couldn't remember what exactly had happened, or claimed that the police misunderstood their statements. Word was that King even took the life of his best friend over a few thousand dollars that went missing.

With each step the man took, I got even more terrified. By the time he was on me, all emotion had given way to a numbness that was beyond words. I went so far past being terrified that I came back to being at peace. I was as close to understanding death as I could be without being in physical jeopardy. All that was missing was the tunnel with the light at the end.

Red briefly glanced at King, shook the dice in his hand, and let them go. His streak continued, and all but two Pharaohs dropped out of the game. "I thought y'all were getting money over here," Red asked. "Y'all ain't getting no money? Y'all don't wanna play no more?"

King stepped into Red's line of sight and said, "You better recognize the King when you see him."

Red stared at King as he blew on the dice and rolled again. They landed at one, two, one: snake eyes. Just like that, his winning streak was over. When we left, Red was happy because he had made a couple hundred dollars in the game. I was just happy to be out of there.

///////////////////

That was the last time I ever hung out with Red. Three weeks later, he was shot two times in the head while getting his car washed at a local hand-wash on one of the 'hood's back blocks. Everyone knew who killed him. Hell, even the police had a good idea. Godfather put a price on the killer's head, but before anyone could cash in, the murderer was behind bars on unrelated charges.

With Red gone, Junior's crew stopped coming around and the guys working under Red lost their direction. Red was the strength. Red would say, "This is what it is: Fuck everything. I don't give a fuck about any of these niggas," and that's what it would be. He fed everyone else. Because he didn't care about obstacles, no one who worked for him did either. If Red was there to say, "We're going down there to see about these niggas," that's what it would have been. Everyone would have gone and done whatever he said. But he couldn't say anything with two holes in his head.

Everyone got scattered. For a while, the strip was open, and while it was open, Baisley started pumping again. Then everybody else started pumping heavy. After a while, everything went back to normal, and the strip was a free zone. Hitting Red was the answer to a lot of people's problems.

///////////////////////////////////

"I kept pulling the trigger until I busted the firing pin . . ."

Not too long after Red got killed, I finally bought my first piece of steel from Old Man Dan. Dan used to walk around with dark sunglasses, a large cowboy hat, and matching boots. He drove a big, bright red Cadillac that had Indian feathers hanging from the rearview mirror. He said he was a cowboy because blacks used to be cowboys. Although no one ever really speaks about black cowboys anymore, they were real, according to Dan. As his way of keeping the legacy of the black cowboy alive, Dan purchased guns out of state and sold them in the 'hood for twice what he paid. I didn't know much about being a black cowboy, but I listened to his history lessons and copped a .380 ACP pistol from him for eight hundred dollars. It was a big investment for me at the time, but it would have cost me more not to have it if someone were to rob me.

Dan used to shoot at a firing range in Long Island, but I was too young to go, so I practiced shooting on the other side of the Conduit, near my grandmother's house. I shot at stationary targets—cans, old toys, basketballs, whatever I could get my hands on. Sometimes a fiend would try to sell me something that I had no use for, but if it would make a decent target, I'd take it. I bought two boxes of shells from Dan and popped the pistol a few times a week. My aim was better than most, but it wasn't anything to brag about. I was pretty sure that I had the heart to shoot a person if necessary, but I wasn't sure if I'd be able to hit my mark when that time came. I would find out soon enough.

///////////////

I met this chick named Tracee while I was shopping for clothes on Jamaica Avenue. It took a few phone calls and a couple of visits to her school, but I finally smooth-talked her into letting me come over for a visit. I was excited because I knew I was going to get some pussy. We had spoken enough to know what the visit would be about without having to say it. I wore some of the freshest clothes I owned. I threw on my 8-Ball jacket, which was a type of multicolored leather jacket with a big number eight on the back that was popular in the early nineties. I threw on brand-new jeans and a spanking-white pair of sneakers. And just to be special, I swiped one of Brian's chains—a thick gold rope with a chunky pendant— off his dresser. I also packed the .380, just in case.

Tracee lived out in the Redfern projects, in Far Rockaway. I took a cab to her house; I was able to pay the driver by the hour, so I had him wait outside for me. I figured I'd be able to go upstairs, get what I wanted, and be back down in enough time to pay the cab for only two hours' worth of time.

The plastic windows to her building's front door had been fogged out by a cigarette lighter, so I wasn't able to see inside the lobby. I didn't think anything of it, because hustlers do that all the time to keep the police from seeing what's going on inside. It wasn't uncommon for the housing police to patrol the projects on mountain bikes and peek into the buildings. Lobbies were always a good place to hustle or hang out in when the temperature got colder. From the inside of the lobby, the street could be seen without having to deal with the weather or the cops. And once the window was smoked out, it was easy to peek outside without being seen.

If I hadn't been so preoccupied with getting some pussy, I would have buttoned up my jacket and been more on point. When I walked into the lobby, my mind was already upstairs so I didn't pay any attention to the two guys hanging out. I just hit the button and went upstairs.

When I came down forty-five minutes later, I was as happy as I could be. But my happiness went away very quickly because it looked like every stickup kid from the project was down in the lobby. Those two dudes must've got on the project's bullhorn and said there was a kid with an 8-Ball jacket and jewelry in the building. They didn't need all of those guys if they really wanted to lay on me. Hell, if the two guys who sent out the alert had any heart, they could've laid on me themselves. I was only sixteen. I was still a little nigga, and I hadn't been on point coming in. But as far as robbers go, these guys were extra-sloppy.

I realized what was going on as soon as I saw the crowd in the lobby. I hot-stepped to the door and was halfway out of the building before any of them realized that I was the kid they were all waiting around to rob. When they saw me, they tried to circle around me, but I was already a few steps away from the door. One of them tried to get me back by calling me over like he knew me. "Yo, come here for a second, man," he said. "Lemme talk to you real quick."

I said, "Nah, man, there ain't nothing for you to talk to me about," and opened the door. My heart was pushing through my chest. When I saw the cab parked at the far end of the courtyard, I cursed myself for thinking with my dick. I heard the bodies spilling out the door behind me. I didn't even have to look. I just felt them on my back. I walked a few feet, hoping they'd just give up in the light of day, but they kept coming. They were getting hungrier and bolder. It felt like they were going to just run on me at any second, so I grabbed the .380 out of my pocket and spun. I didn't look, I didn't think. I just let off all six shots I had in the gun. I kept pulling the trigger until I busted the firing pin. Then I ran to the cab.

Later that night, Tracee called me, checking to see if I was okay. I told her that I was and asked her why she was checking on me. At that point, I didn't have much experience with girls, so I didn't realize that I should have called her after having sex with her. But she wanted to talk. After a while, she asked me if I had seen anything when I was leaving the building. I told her I hadn't. Then she told me that a kid had gotten shot in the leg in front of her building earlier that afternoon and she was glad that I hadn't been around. I told her it was a crazy world, but I was glad I missed the shooting because I could have been just walking along, minding my own business, and caught a bullet. She said that she was glad nothing happened to me and asked when she'd see me again. I told her that I'd see her soon, but I was lying. I stopped taking her calls and never went to see her again. No piece of pussy was worth getting jumped for.

////////////////////

After Tracee, I started going out with Tasha. I met Tasha through Ray-Ray's girlfriend, Nicci, and she became my first real girlfriend. She lived on

Rockaway Boulevard, which was close enough for me not to worry about getting robbed or shooting anyone when I went to see her but far enough away for me to continue to play the field. I was still new to the girl game, and I wound up putting more money than time into the relationship. I'd take her out once in a while, but for the most part, I'd just buy her shoes and clothes and stuff. All that really mattered to me was that she was there when I needed some pussy. Having a girlfriend, even if I was tricking on her, was a lot easier than chasing down chicks all the time.

One night, Ray-Ray called to say that we should take Tasha and Nicci on a double date. I was making money on the block, so I passed. Ray-Ray was like, "You'd rather get money than be with your girlfriend?"

"You damned straight," I said. "You wanna be in love, you can go ahead and be in love. I'd rather be in money."

The thing is, Ray-Ray never told me that he was talking to me on a speakerphone with Tasha and Nicci in the room. I didn't find that part out until months later. But because I had said some slick shit on the phone, Tasha wound up going to the movies that night with Brian's little brother, John. After the movie, they got two rooms at a motel around the way. Tasha figured that since I would rather be in money, she'd let someone else be in her and wound up fucking John.

No one told me about this shit for months. I was still tricking on her, buying her clothes and shoes and stuff, and John was fucking her behind my back. It wasn't until I bought her an expensive shearling coat for Christmas that Brian stepped in to regulate the situation. Brian didn't know about what was going on at first, but once he did, he told John that waiting until I found out about the situation on my own was only going to make things worse.

John was so scared to confess that he brought Brian with him when he was ready to tell me. He swore that he only messed with Tasha a few times after that first night and then left her alone, but I didn't really care. I liked Tasha, but really, she was just kind of there to be there. I didn't like the idea of getting played, but a ho's going to be a ho. There's not much that can be done about something like that. I just told John to pay me the five hundred dollars I had spent on the coat. He was like, *All I gotta do is pay $500?* Everyone seemed to think I was going to go crazy or something, but I wasn't. I just took my money and left. Then I called Tasha to come over to my grandmother's house. When she got there, I stripped the coat off her back and told her to go home in the cold. I couldn't get back all the money I had spent on her, but I damned sure wasn't going to let her run around in that coat. That soured me on women for a while. They just weren't worth the effort.

*"My heart dropped.
It was like I was seeing a ghost . . ."*

I caught the gambling bug right before my first year of high school. I was hot on the dice. In one night, I won fifty-six hundred dollars in the alley on the strip. The next day, I went to the Kawasaki shop on Jamaica Avenue and bought a Ninja 600 ZX-6R. No plates, no insurance, no registration. I just drew some numbers on a piece of cardboard and placed that on the back in lieu of a license plate and parked it in the street and everything like it was legal. I rode the bike to school every morning and parked it at Brian's house at night because I didn't want my grandmother to know about it. She still didn't know that I was selling drugs.

I didn't really think anything about my high school's metal detectors. I never carried a gun to school and when I carried a knife, I would stash it outside in the bushes or somewhere on my motorcycle. The screening process was random; they didn't pick everyone to be searched. That would have been impossible, and no one would ever have gotten to class. Instead, they would pick the guys who looked like they would start something and the girls who might smuggle something in for those guys. I got searched a lot, so I was sure never to bring any weapons to school.

The security guard placed my bag on the table and started searching, digging deep through everything. I was joking with him, like, "If you find any money in there, let me know." He didn't pay me any mind. He was one of those guys who's just focused on his job and nothing else. He was quick and thorough, and he went through my stuff like he was a machine. First, he took all my books out of my book bag and set them on the table. Then, he searched every nook and cranny of the bag and began to replace the stuff in the bag. He opened and shook each notebook. I figured there must have been a lot of kids coming to school with hollowed-out textbooks and razors taped inside loose-leaf binders. I thought this guy was ridiculous, so I was still joking with him as he finished up. "You're doing a pretty good job there," I said. "Maybe when you're done, you can come and clean my room for me. Do you do windows?"

He continued to ignore me. The only things left to put back in my bag were my sneakers. He dug deep inside and pulled a sock out. Then he tapped the heels together. A bunch of green tops rolled out. My heart dropped. It was like I was seeing a ghost. And in a way, I was. The pieces were old. It had been months since I used green tops. They were the first caps I used after Red died, but I had been moving gold-topped illusions for some time. I had stashed the green tops in those sneakers so my grandmother couldn't find them. I cursed myself for picking up the wrong pair of sneakers. I couldn't believe it.

Between spending time in the dean's office, being processed at the precinct, and waiting in Central Booking to see the judge for possession of a controlled substance, I had plenty of time to think about my mistake. In my mind, the only reason I got caught was because I was hiding the drugs from my grandmother. It's like I was being punished for abusing her trust. I had hidden the pieces so well that I wound up hiding them from myself. Had I told her what was going on, I wouldn't have been run through the system—at least not for carrying crack to school.

When Brian picked me up that night, I had him drop me off at school so I could ride my bike home. My grandparents were waiting up for me. They sat me down. They didn't know much outside of what happened except that I had been arrested. I'm not sure how they found out without my telling them, but it didn't matter. I was going to tell them anyway. When they began talking to me, I realized that they thought I used drugs. I had to let them know the truth. "I don't use drugs," I said. "I sell drugs. If you're gonna put me out, put me out."

It wasn't until I told my grandmother that I was selling drugs that she finally explained what happened to my mother. Until then, we had never had a conversation about her. When my mother died, my grandfather was the one who told me that she wasn't coming back, that she had died in her sleep. That had taken a while to sink in, because at that point, she wasn't constantly physically present in my life. I understood that she was hustling. I saw what she did as work. Even then I knew that it wouldn't be smart for me to be up under her when she was grinding. She had to get out there and be in the middle of things, where it was popping, and that wasn't a good place for me to be. She hadn't been present, but she put me up in the best way she could and provided for me financially.

I'm not sure how my grandmother felt about my mom's lifestyle or when she found out. I know it had to hurt to have to bury her own daughter. And I think that's why she didn't tell me what had happened. I used to think that it was because I was too young to understand, but as time went on I realized that my grandmother needed to not say it just as much as she wanted to protect me. It's much harder to explain death to an eight-year-old than it is to someone who's older. She just gave me bits and pieces of information until I told her that I was selling drugs. Then she told me everything.

My grandfather didn't say a word. He got up and walked out of the room. Then my grandmother told me that my mother had been murdered. She said that she herself had never gotten all of the details. Because my mom had lived her life apart from the rest of the family, the story had to be pieced together. Most of what my grandmother knew came from official records—police investigations, the coroner's report—mixed with a bit of common sense and whatever my aunts and uncles were able to find out.

My mother had been at home when someone slipped something in her drink to make her fall asleep. The murderer then closed all the windows in her house and turned on the gas from the stove.

My grandmother apologized for failing me; she thought that it was her fault that I chose to sell drugs. I didn't know what to say. Even now, as I think about my reasons for dealing, it may sound like I'm putting it on her. The truth is that I made my choice on my own. I wanted things and I knew she couldn't give them to me. I couldn't even ask for those things with a straight face. What I was being told back then about getting money didn't make any sense to me. I was already having a hard time in school, but I was supposed to stay in school for another six years—without college. With college, I was looking at ten years easy. So after a decade, I'd be able to get a good job and work and get the things I wanted. But when I looked around the neighborhood, I saw people who were getting the things they wanted in six months from hustling. Hustling didn't seem like one of the options, it seemed like the only option.

In a way, I was my mother's son. Seeing her getting money from hustling at a young age definitely altered me. The people I used to see her with were the same kinds of people who turned me on to the game. They were the people who appeared to have things, and they were the ones I felt comfortable asking for things. But when I told those guys that I was hungry, they didn't give me a fish, they gave me a fishing pole. That's what Sincere did when he gave me those first coke pieces. And I came to understand that that's what Brian was trying to protect me from.

That night, talking to my grandmother, I had nothing to say. She had lost a daughter to drugs and her children were either addicts or married to dealers. Now even her grandchild had taken to pushing crack cocaine. It hurt me to hear her blame herself for my decision. Still, it took a weight off my shoulders for her to know what I was doing. At least it meant that I could stop lying to her. And because I wouldn't have to hide my dealing from her anymore, I'd be able to get more work done. That's what I told myself, and that's the way it was.

"You can go to jail for that shit . . ."

After I was caught with the pieces in school, I was suspended from the New York City public school system for two weeks. During those two weeks, I pumped crack night and day. When I was reinstated in a new high school, I continued to pump crack night and day. After the judicial system sentenced me to eighteen month's probation, I continued to pump crack night and day. Nothing that happened to me changed that.

School became a fashion show at that point. I would show up only when I had new clothes to wear: Oh, I got some fresh shit to wear? I'ma go to school on Thursday. Formal schooling wasn't necessary for me. It had lost whatever attraction it held about the time I copped my first brick from Carlos. From that, I learned the most important numbers for my day. I could break down a kilogram of cocaine into ounces, grams, or any combination of the two. That's how I learned my fractions and metric conversion, through real-life applications. With my confession to my grandmother, school's usefulness as a cover story had come to an end. There was really no loss on my part. My favorite subjects rarely had anything to do with the subject itself—it had more to do with the teacher. If a teacher left me alone, or bothered me at a level I could at least tolerate, then that was a good subject for me.

I always took a liking to social studies, though, mainly world history—war and shit like that. War had interested me from my earliest days, since I used to play with those green army men. I really got excited about the strategy and the fights between good and evil, like, We're right and they're wrong, so we have to get rid of them. How could you make that boring? A lot of teachers did, however. They turned war into a game of numbers, dates, and who signed what piece of paper. I was like, What happened to the part about getting rid of the other guy for the good of the world? School just made everything corny.

So it's no surprise that I went back to the strip. What was a surprise was that Reg was on the strip, too. Reg was Brian's younger brother, but he had no business being on the strip; the nigga still smelled of jail. When the cops came to pick us up, they probably smelled the past six years of the Big House on him. They musta been like, *You have the right to remain silent. If you choose not to remain silent, anything you say can and will be used against . . . wait up, nigga, you smell just like Virginia's Baskerville Correctional Center!*

When someone comes out of jail, the parole board will suggest that he change his environment—his people, places, and things. Otherwise, the ex-con is going to wind up right back in jail. It's really simple. But Reg had never known anything about a legal job, and selling drugs was the closest thing he had to a marketable skill. Nothing he learned during his six-year vacation had changed that. Like any recently released convict who hadn't changed his stripes, Reg was playing catch-up, soaking up the tales of the years gone by, trying to get back in the groove.

We were just out there on the boulevard—Reg, Brian, and myself. Shawn was across the street. I had just come from a probation meeting, so I didn't have any work on me. Brian had moved beyond hand-to-hand sales. Reg was too fresh out of the pen to have been set up. The only one with work was Shawn, Mr. I don't care. A man none of us had ever seen before came over. He asked Brian for some crack. Brian was indignant and screamed, "Man, get the fuck away from me!" First off, he was wary of a new fiend. Moreover, he was insulted that the guy assumed he was a street vendor. Then the man walked over to Reg, who sent the man to Shawn, posted across the street. Reg was thinking, I could definitely get into this new way of dealing. Customers just walk up to you as you stand minding your own business!

"You can't do that, man!" I told Reg. "You can go to jail for that shit."

The man crossed over to Shawn and copped twenty dollars' worth of vials. Reg was like, "Go to jail? For what? I ain't got shit on me."

I had to explain to this nigga that the laws had changed. For what he just did, Reg could have caught a steering charge. He didn't have to have anything on him; he could be picked up for being an accessory to the sale. There was a whole lot of new shit going on that he wasn't up on. Before Reg went in, there was no TNT, no buy-and-bust program. In six years, the rule of possession had changed—he could even be arrested for being in proximity to a stash, as long as the cops could prove that it was his, which wasn't really hard once they got to spreading their bullshit on the stand. They'd have reports noting that they observed him going back and forth to the hiding spot all day, even if he had only opened up shop a few minutes prior. I was about to school him on mandatory sentencing guidelines when two unmarked cars rolled up on the strip like possessed pigs with undercover narcs spilling out, guns drawn, ordering everyone to their knees. *You have the right to remain silent. If you choose not to remain silent, anything you say can and will be used against . . . wait up, nigga, you smell just like Virginia's Baskerville Correctional Center!*

The shit was crazy. Brian disavowed any knowledge of anything whatsoever. He was just standing on the street and, last time he checked, it was a free country and standing on the street was not a crime—that was his story and he was sticking to it so hard the arresting officers couldn't pry him off of it with a crowbar. They took him down to the precinct anyway and let him off with a desk-appearance ticket for loitering or disorderly conduct or some other dumb misdemeanor when they couldn't find a lie to stick on him.

I tried the same tactic as Brian. I was just standing on the street and, last time I checked, it was a free country and standing on the street was not a crime. They told me I'd have to explain it to the judge. I was like, What the fuck? How come this nigga gets off and I don't? I found out why that night during a preliminary hearing, when the state laid its case:

"What we have here, Your Honor, is one of the many highly evolved crack cells that are operating throughout the neighborhood of South Jamaica, Queens. One guy acts as a lookout, one person steers the customer and sometimes handles the money, while a third deals with the actual sale. In some cases, the lookout or the steerer will also have weapons on their person in order to ward off rival cells. In this case, the lookout and the steerer were clean, but the State maintains that they were all operating in accord nonetheless. It's really quite simple; it happens all the time. The menacing plague of crack throughout the city has birthed many of these little cottage operations. The State would like to take this matter to trial and rid the city streets of these brazen street dealers. Only by putting such men behind bars can the threat of deadly, murderous crack gangs be held at bay."

I pleaded not guilty through my court-appointed lawyer. "Defendant Curtis Jackson was just standing on the street, talking to a friend, when he was unlawfully apprehended by the police in a gross violation of his civil rights," my attorney said. "These charges are without merit. Furthermore, the defense would like to bring charges of brutality and abuse against the arresting officers." *Yeah! That's what I was talking about! Minding my own business. Illegal arrest. Brutality. God bless America!*

But the State countered that the innocent bystander was recorded by an undercover officer. Five choice words—"You can't do that, man!"—were caught on tape by the undercover officer. "Your Honor, Defendant Curtis Jackson is not only an accessory to the crime," the prosecutor said, "he is an integral part of a cell operating within a larger drug network in the neighborhood and should not be let back on the streets." The judge adjourned the case to trial and released me to the custody of my grandmother. She was in the back row of the courtroom. Crying.

IIIIIₐₐₐₐₐₐIIIII

In the weeks leading up to the trial, the court's paperwork coalesced into some damaging evidence regarding Defendant Jackson: "It would seem that less than six months ago, Defendant Jackson was arrested for carrying crack cocaine to his high school—in his sneaker, no less. During his probation period, the repeat offender was given to failing urinalysis exams with the same fervor that he is now failing the game of life, Your Honor. In fact, less than three weeks before his most recent arrest, Defendant Jackson tested positive during one of the routine urine tests stipulated by the terms of his probation. It would seem that Defendant Jackson not only sells drugs but is using them as well."

What was I supposed to say? *No, what happens is I spend days on end manufacturing and packaging crack cocaine. I am so into making crack that sometimes I eat lunch while cutting boulders into pebbles, and I push them into vials without washing my hands. I don't wear gloves or anything because the health inspectors don't come around that often. It's obvious that the residue got into my bloodstream. It's all a simple misunderstanding, see?*

Nah, that was cool by me. It hurt to be viewed as a common crackhead, but it would have been stupid to confess to greater charges. I explained to my attorney that I had cooked a little crack, not mentioning that a little amounted to about a quarter kilo every few days. At any rate, my attorney didn't find it wise to use that defense in court. It would be half a decade before authorities would accept the fact that cocaine base is so fine and resilient that it easily binds to the ink of a dollar bill. So the argument that an estimated four of every five bills of U.S. currency contains trace levels of coca powder was not presented at that time. As far as the record was concerned, Defendant Jackson was a drug user. Defendant Jackson could live with that. The State offered Defendant Jackson three years' probation. Defendant Jackson could live with that as well. My co-defendants were another story.

Of all people to be locked into a case with, I had two guys who spent more time in jail than they did on the streets. Thing was, Shawn's and Reg's attitudes toward incarceration were night and day. Shawn—the only one of us who actually did have drugs on him at the time of the arrest—was all *I don't care.* He was offered a term of one to three years for criminal possession and sale of a controlled substance in various degrees. He could live with that. Hell, he didn't care. His attorney had a hard time figuring out what Shawn was saying. "You do realize that this arrest constitutes a violation of your parole and you'll have to serve time for the violation as well? I may be able to get the time to run concurrent but . . ."

"I don't care."

Reg, on the other hand, was not willing to go back to jail. He was charged as an accessory and offered time served by the State. But a guilty plea would put him in violation of his parole, so he would be sent back to Virginia no sooner than the judge's gavel concluded the case. He wouldn't even leave the courtroom. The bailiffs would hold him in State custody until federal marshals could be there to take him to Virginia. He would be bounced from one holding facility to another for a few weeks before anyone would know where to find him. And chances were very likely that his final resting spot would be right back in Virginia's Baskerville Correctional Center.

Reg said thanks but no thanks to the State's gracious proposition. It made sense—he had just come home and was not looking forward to going back. We understood what it was: He had just done six years, he did not want to go back. But because we were all codefendants, his unwillingness to cop out made our situations worse.

We had to take the case to trial in the Queens Supreme Court, and we tried every trick in the book. Our lawyers motioned for a Mapp hearing to suppress the evidence, claiming the wiretap was illegal. We had a Huntley hearing, saying that statements obtained by the police in the precinct were in violation of procedure. When the prosecutors saw that we were willing to drag out the proceedings to no end, they put a new deal on the table: A one-year term for Reg, two to four for Shawn, and twenty-two months in a court-mandated drug-rehabilitation program for me. I was like, "Twenty-two months? What happened to the probation deal?"

My attorney said, "That was before you guys decided to waste everybody's time with legal tricks, which I told you wouldn't work."

Reg was still down to fight it, but his lawyer convinced him to take the deal. The deals would only get worse as time went on, and the State doesn't take kindly to people who turn down its offers. They really hold that shit against you. I learned not to play with the courts when it comes to those deals. Fucking around took me from three years of running free and pissing in a cup to two years locked up in a court-mandated drug-rehabilitation program. *And what the fuck was a court-mandated drug-rehabilitation program anyway?*

I'd find out soon enough.

"This right here is your last chance.
Next stop, the Big House . . ."

The Program was housed in a small Brooklyn apartment building that had been re-envisioned into a "safe space" where you could "rise from the ashes of your fears" through the power of tax dollars. The first level contained executive offices, several small meeting areas, a kitchen, and a cafeteria. The upstairs was remodeled as a dormitory. Women lived on the pink-colored second floor and guys stayed on the blue third level. There were seven rooms on each floor. You could get to the dorms through two separate stairways; the one on the left was for the girls and led to the second floor, the one on the right gave access to the guys' level. Two people were assigned to a room. Each room had two twin-size beds, two small desks, and one dresser that was shared by the people staying in the room. And everywhere—outside the rooms, in the hallways, by the stairs, at the entrance to the bathroom—were the rules:

NO YELLING.
RUNNING PROHIBITED.
TURN LIGHTS OFF WHEN NOT IN USE.
CIGARETTES, ALCOHOL, AND DRUGS ARE STRICTLY
PROHIBITED.
LOVE YOURSELF.
FAILURE TO ABIDE BY THE RULES MAY RESULT IN
EXPULSION FROM THE HOUSE AND PROGRAM.

The court-mandated, city-regulated Program didn't have any bars. Just rules. Lots of them. And if you broke any, you'd be sent to the place with bars. It was really that simple. The counselors spoke the good shit about love and the merits of acceptance and forgiveness, but they were always ready to intimidate with the quick threat of jail. There'd be a whole bunch of talk about loving and understanding yourself, lectures on realizing the power within you, and suggestions that you'd have to change your people, places, and things in order to distance yourself from toxic relationships. But when things got rough, it was, "Keep fuckin' around and you'll be in jail faster than it takes for you to smoke a rock of crack." I saw that support and acceptance were the primary strategy, but when a participant became unruly or noncompliant, then all the bullshit hit the fan and the big guns came out: "Listen, buddy, you've already fucked up your life. This right here is your last chance. Next stop, the Big House."

The Program was set up so incoming participants would share a room with longer-standing residents, who played the role of a big brother or sister. The big sibling's role was to teach the new resident the ins and outs of the Program—you know, how to follow the rules. My big brother did what he was supposed to: He instructed me in the ways of residency, even though everything had been explained to me during orientation and would be repeated every morning, noon, and night during the Program. The theory was that recovering addicts could relate more to one of their own and that the big sibling would turn the black-and-white plainness of the Program literature into a living action plan. "We can't teach you love," the counselors would say. "We can only show you where it is: inside of yourself."

There was a lot of bullshit flying in that place. The truth is the staff was just coasting by without doing anything while the big siblings did everything. Good thing, then, that there was big brother Ed. Ed was this older white guy who had four months left in the Program. He was appointed to "guide me through the initial stages of withdrawal and into acceptance." Ed was real cool. After such a long time in the Program, he was just ready to return to his life. He realized that the Program served a purpose, though not as well as everyone seemed to think it did. Ed said that he had fallen into a hole and the Program helped him to climb out, but only because he wanted to get out of the hole in the first place.

"If I go back to smoking that rock, it'll only be because I've given up on my life," he said. "At that point, I'm dead. I'd have to have nothing to live for and would just be waiting for my days to end." He would say this over and over in many different ways, whether it was in our room or at meetings. Ed blamed no one but himself. He said that personal responsibility had been his weakest asset, but he had become aware of his own power and it was now his greatest strength. He could make the life that he chose, and that was exactly what he was going to do when he left the Program. He had already worked to the point where he was granted leave privileges and allowed to get a full-time job as a stockperson in a supermarket. "You don't belong here, Curtis," he told me. "You're not the type of kid that lets life get to you. I can see it in your eyes."

I told him that I never used drugs. I told him that I sold drugs, but not how much. Ed understood and said that he didn't blame me. He just felt that I was misdirected. "Determined, but misdirected," he said. "Dealers don't break people. People break themselves. The dealers just make use of the pieces because there's nothing else for them to take advantage of. Drug dealers aren't predators. They're scavengers, circling overhead like vultures waiting for the last light of life to be gone from their mark. Only then will they swoop down and feast on the remains." For Ed, it all came down to personal responsibility.

I thought a lot about what he said. If someone else had been my big brother, I don't think I would have been able to tell him the truth. But Ed was real cool and he didn't make me feel fucked-up for selling crack. That made me think even more. I had never seen crack fiends as anything more than customers. Even though some of my own family members had become addicts, I never knew fiends past their habit and buying patterns. My time in rehab did a lot to change that. I wasn't about to stop dealing crack. Not by a long shot. But I was going to learn to do it better.

The shares always took place downstairs in one of the meeting rooms. Downstairs was decorated with advertisements for city services; most were printed in both Spanish and English. There was a dog in a trench coat saying that good citizens should "Take a Bite Out of Crime." Propaganda for Crime Stoppers, with the toll-free snitch hotlines (1-800-577-TIPS or, *en español*, 1-888-57-PISTA), was prominently displayed. Pictures of missing children were plastered everywhere. Other ads provided support information for alcoholism, drug addiction, domestic abuse, depression, and more. It seemed like if it could go wrong in society, there was a hotline for it, and that hotline was advertised on that first floor. The meeting rooms were wallpapered with motivational posters. I'M FREE TO CHOOSE LIFE OR DEATH . . . THE JOURNEY OF A THOUSAND MILES BEGINS WITH ONE STEP . . . BE YOURSELF, BUT BE YOUR BEST SELF . . . NOW IS THE TIME . . . the one about God walking with the guy on the beach . . . and the Program's favorite, EITHER YOU'RE PART OF THE PROBLEM OR YOU'RE PART OF THE SOLUTION.

I was always invited to share, but I hardly ever did. What was I supposed to say? *Hey, I'm Curtis and I'm sorry that y'all lives are fucked-up. But if you ever decide to go back to smoking when you get out, come to me. I'll be right on the same strip that I was picked up at—that's Guy R. Brewer Boulevard and 134th Street in Queens—because as soon as I get out of here, I'm going right back to selling crack. And now that I've seen how deeply addictive, and therefore profitable, heroin is, I'll be selling that as well. And when they come out with some new shit to sell, I'll be selling that, too. Ask for Boo.*

I wasn't in the least bit rehabilitated. Nor was I going to be. The Program was geared for broken souls and damaged minds. I was neither. And my incompatibility quickly began to show. During my first week, I was given a small pamphlet to memorize. It contained the house's cardinal rules, a 12-step platform, and notes on responsibility. I was able to commit the booklet to memory in under twenty minutes. This caused conflict. The counselors knew that I could repeat the phrases, but they were like, "Did you allow those words to get into your heart?" Other participants took weeks—sometimes months—to learn the material.

"That's because they're all crackheads," I'd say. "I'm not a crackhead. I don't need to keep rereading this shit to figure it out." From the jump, the counselors could see that I was going to be a problem. Not only was I uncooperative, full of anger, cussing, and using forbidden terminology ("crackhead"), but I was also in denial. That was the answer for everything: denial. If someone didn't take to the Program, it's because he was in denial. As far as they were concerned, I was in Denial Level Ten. If anyone ever needed the Program, it was me. And if I stayed in denial long enough, I'd be sent to jail.

"Maybe you should read the pamphlet again."

"I told you, I already read it."

"Well, maybe you should read it again."

What the . . . ?

For a full hour three times a day, the group would meet to read and discuss the pamphlet. While the group read in silence, I just damned myself for saying those five words—"You can't do that, man!"—to Reg. I replayed the incident in my mind. Sometimes I would let Reg be arrested. Sometimes I'd wait for the officer to go across the street to Shawn before I schooled Reg. Sometimes I would tell the cop to go to hell, just like Brian had. But mostly I would just daydream. I'd listen to a motorcycle racing past outside and think back to riding my bike to school. Whenever a counselor interrupted my stream of thought, I'd quote a passage from the pamphlet word for word, and then turn back to daydreaming.

The night before Ed left, I asked him how he managed to make it through the Program. He closed his eyes and recited a poem he had learned:

> *In life you'll make mistakes, as we all will do,*
> *And it seems like you don't have enough to even make due—*
> *Your faith may be low, and the tide real high,*
> *And you can't get above water no matter how hard you try.*
> *If you feel at the end and say, "This is it,"*
> *Stop and take a breather, but just don't quit.*
> *Your journey may be full of twists and curves,*
> *But if you hold on tight, you can make it through the swerves.*
> *If you stay the course when you're down and out,*
> *You may be amazed at how quickly things turn around.*
> *Don't give up before the race is done,*
> *Just take one step—and then another one.*
> *The end is near, though it appears to be far,*
> *You'll be surprised to know how close you are.*
> *Here's something to recall when your path is darkest lit:*
> *It's always darkest before the dawn,*
> *And you can make it if you just don't quit.*

Fine, I thought. I'm stuck here. And I can't quit because quitting means going to jail. I had to figure something out.

From that night, my outlook on the Program changed. I realized that I couldn't beat the Program, so my best bet was to join it—or at least appear to join it. The only way out of the game was to play it and play it to win. I became an astute observer of the counselors. I paid attention to what they liked and what they didn't like. I filed all the information and took on the behaviors that would be viewed as *compliance* and therefore be rewarded. It worked. The counselors remarked that I was making exceptional progress and began to hold me up as the poster child for acceptance. "Look at Curtis," they'd say. "He's been able to turn everything around by taking responsibility for his actions. You should all do the same."

I fooled the counselors easy enough, but the Program's participants were another matter. They held no power over me and I didn't feel the need to play along for them. They hated me for that. They'd really let me have it when it came to Confrontation. Confrontation was organized similar to Shares, except that Confrontation allowed participants to air out our beefs. During Confrontation, the rules against cussing were suspended—anything short of physical attack was allowed. Man, those crackheads would really get in my face and let loose. One time, this one guy really let me have it. He kept going on and on, like he was running for president or something:

"*Curtis breaks all of the house rules when no one is looking. Curtis runs and skips on the steps. Curtis always shows up late when he's on kitchen duty. Curtis is not helpful. Curtis has a negative attitude that makes working with him hard. One time he was skipping on the steps and I told him that he wasn't supposed to do that and you know what he told me? He told me, 'Look, I'm a pro at this. I been skippin' steps since I could walk.' Curtis is not part of the solution. Curtis is part of the problem.*"

"Would you like to reply, Curtis?"

Yes, I thought. I'd like to reply with a fuckin' brick upside this fuckin' guy's head. Is it okay if I just take him outside and reply personally? But I remembered Ed's poem. Quitting was bullshit. "I'm sorry if I made you feel that way," I said. "It wasn't my intention. I'll work to keep your feelings in mind as I go about my day. From now on, I'm going to be more responsible. I don't want to be part of the problem. I want to be part of the solution."

That night after dinner, I was running up the steps three at a time. The guy who had called me out earlier called to me. "Ah-ah-ah," he said. "Curtis, you're running up the steps again."

I came up on this guy's face. "I told you not to tell me nothin' about runnin' up no fuckin' steps."

"But you said you wanted to be part of the solution, remember?"

"Oh that? Let me tell you what it is. If you said that shit to me in the street, I would put your head through a wall. But I can't do that here. So anytime you call me on that bullshit, I'm gonna do just like I did today. I'm gonna get up and say all the shit the counselors wanna hear. And while I'm saying that shit, I'ma look at your feet, then I'ma look at your eyes. Then I'ma look at your feet, then I'ma look at your eyes. For some reason, they buy that shit. Look, I'ma do it right now just for practice." I began to apologize to the guy for running up the steps. I looked at his feet. Then his eyes. Then his feet. Then his eyes. The guy's face turned as blank as a new sheet of paper. He walked away before I could finish "Where you goin'?" I laughed. "I wasn't finished. C'mon. Are you gonna be part of the problem or part of the solution, buddy?"

Most of the remainder of my stay in the Program went according to plan. In meetings, I was called on for advice ("I really think that Linda just has to let go and let in God") or to lead the group in prayer ("God, grant me the serenity to accept the things I cannot change, the courage to change the things I can, and the wisdom to know the difference"). Then I'd run up the stairs. To the counselors, I was the model participant; to the participants, I was a con artist. It was all good—until Ms. Jaworski came along.

Ms. Jaworski took over the Program from its previous director. She was a hands-on type and wanted to get to know all the participants. Before she came, I didn't even realize the Program had a director. The former director just stayed in her office, took meetings, did interviews, and, once in a while, took a small group of politician types on a tour of the house. Jaworski, on the other hand, wanted to be a big part of the Program's day-to-day operations. Behind her desk was a plaque that read THE PRICE OF SUCCESS IS DEDICATION, HARD WORK, AND AN UNREMITTING DEVOTION TO SEE THE THINGS YOU WANT TO SEE HAPPEN.

/////////////

Ms. Jaworski quickly recognized me for the bullshit artist that I was. First off, she recommended that my stay in the Program be extended. She also suggested that my upcoming leave privileges would be suspended until I came to grips with my addiction and realized that I couldn't get through life by fooling everyone around me. She claimed that she had seen too many families broken by drugs and too many treatment centers turned into places with revolving-door policies. Our new director said that she was as sure that the sun was in the sky that the Program would become a bastion of glory under her tenure.

"All that's fine and good," I said. "But I got sent here because I *sold* drugs. I now realize that I was wrong to do so and I'm just eager to return to my family and become a productive member of society."

"You can lay it on as thick as you want," she said. "You can do that little trick where you look at the floor then shine me with those puppy-dog eyes all you want. But until I believe you're truly rehabilitated, you're going to stay right here." She gave me a long lecture on responsibility, then filled out my report. "Participant is in denial and refuses to comply with the program."

Her stroke of the pen nearly sent me over the edge. I was like, *No fucking way, bitch. I'll put a brick in your head!* Keeping my anger in check has never been my strong point, but I thought about Ed's poem: "Here's something to recall when your path is darkest lit: / It's always darkest before the dawn, / And you can make it if you just don't quit." I said, "I'm not sure what you're talking about, Miss. I am complying with the program to the best of my ability. If there is someplace where you think I could improve, please let me know because I'd really like to become a better person."

"You can get out of my office," she said. "Come back once you've learned to truly appreciate the opportunity you've been given here."

No way was I going to change course when I was this close to getting home. My bullshit had worked on everyone else, so I knew there was something to it. Besides, if I switched up at this stage in the game, not only would the staff not trust me, but they'd make my life hell for fooling them. Then they'd get me sent to jail, just for good measure. I decided that one monkey don't stop no show. I kept up with my award-winning performances, right up until my scheduled court date.

It was a matter of procedure. I had to stand before the judge who sent me to the Program before I was allowed leave privileges. Then I would have to see him again right before my release. For all intents and purposes, it was a formality. The judge would warn me as to what would become of me if I ever showed up in his courtroom again, and then he would send me on my way. But Ms. Jaworski's comments on my report made things a bit more complicated. Judge Rothstein was stunned. Here was a young man making steady progress in the court-mandated program, as well he should, but the most recent entries seemed to counter eighteen months' worth of evaluations.

"I'm not sure what that's about, Your Honor," I said. "I think the new director has it in for me, sir. She's quite stern. I feel as though I am rehabilitated and ready to return to society, sir. Sometimes it seemed that my path was darkly lit. But I know that it's always darkest before the dawn and that I can make it as long as I don't quit, sir." The judge was confused. In his eyes, I was a model graduate. He adjourned the case until the following week, when Ms. Jaworski could come in to explain herself.

"I don't believe that the participants in the program are taking advantage of the opportunity they have been presented with," she told the judge. "They seem to believe that just being present is enough to merit their dismissal. I disagree. And many participants—Curtis Jackson being a prime example—are under the impression that they can charm their way through rehabilitation. I feel that the spirit of the Program is diminished by such participants and I refuse to sign off on their less-than-genuine performance."

Judge Rothstein asked her how long she had been running the program. It was one of those questions he already knew the answer to, but he wanted to let her set herself up for the kill. "Six weeks," she told him.

"So you're telling me that in six weeks you have been able to deduce the superficiality of an ongoing program that has been serving this city for the past four years?" he asked. "You're telling me that we've all been wasting precious time and tax dollars to house, entertain, and vacation drug addicts. You're telling me that we've been getting the wool pulled over our eyes. You're telling me that countless studies and statistics have been wrong. And you're telling me that you were able to see through this charade in a mere six weeks."

She had nothing to say. I had to use every bit of strength I had to keep from laughing.

"Well," the judge said, "I suggest that you amend your evaluation to allow your participant his leave privileges, because if you don't, I will."

////////,,,,,,,,///////

On my first day of leave, I was back on Guy R. Brewer Boulevard—back on the strip. I didn't show up with the exact intention of selling drugs, but it was all I knew. After two years in captivity, I was eager to return to normalcy. The Program had instructed me to stay away from the old and forge the new, and perhaps there was something to that. The players had changed positions and circumstances and the money was not what it had once been. Due to programs and education in schools, there were very few crackheads being made. The market had been tapped.

From the strip, I went to Brian's house. In his bedroom, boxes of sneakers and stacks of clothes were everywhere. His closet was filled with outfits wrapped in plastic from the dry cleaner's. Jewelry was laid out on the dresser next to pictures of Brian posed in front of airbrushed backgrounds. In one photo, he was surrounded by a bunch of guys with velour Gucci suits and leather goose bombers, holding bottles of Derekagne and showing off their jewelry. Another showed him surrounded by three cute girls in front of a big cartoon of Bugs Bunny. A plastic bag of single dollar bills rested atop the TV set, which was attached to a gaming system and a laser-disc player. Brian pulled a gym bag from his closet and poured out a blizzard of cash. The bed was filled with small bills—fives, tens, and twenties. I had never seen so much money in my life. Not even on TV. "That must be a million fuckin' dollars!"

Brian laughed and told me it was one hundred and sixty grand. It wasn't a million dollars, but it was still more money than I could conceive of. I tried to ask how he got so much money, but only wind came out. I was speechless. Me. Speechless.

Brian pushed aside the money like dirty laundry. He sat on a corner of the bed and explained that he had begun to work for Godfather. Godfather had become so powerful that he was able to keep himself far away from direct dealings. It was the best thing for him to do at that point. There was a lot of tension developing between the local distributors and the guys who supplied wholesale cocaine. A lot of deals were going bad. A few Colombian suppliers who were coming down to make deals with people in the 'hood had disappeared; others were robbed. Brian knew for a fact that some guys from the projects had killed at least one Colombian, because they were running their mouths about it before word hit the streets. That was the thing about the underworld—everything that was supposed to be a secret really wasn't. Reputation is the cornerstone of power; there could be no reputation if everything was a secret.

Godfather's rep was that of a sharp businessman, and killing his supplier wouldn't have been good for business. He was more or less exempt from the shady dealings, but regardless, Godfather didn't want to meet with the Colombians and the Colombians didn't want to meet with Godfather. But Godfather needed coke and the Colombians loved profit. The solution was to have Brian deal with the Colombians on Godfather's behalf.

The Colombians charged fifteen thousand dollars per kilo of cocaine. For three weeks straight, Brian picked up twenty bricks from the Colombians, which he turned over to Godfather at the price of eighteen thousand dollars each. That came to sixty thousand dollars a week for three straight weeks, just for being in the middle of the transaction. Brian explained that he had spent some of his money just having fun. He never got change when he went out. Some places, like movie theaters and tollbooths, wouldn't keep the extra money, so if he had singles when he came home, he would just throw them in a plastic bag. He said that he had a garbage bag and a half full of dollar bills that he'd take to the bank when he had time.

From that moment, there was no way you could tell me that I was going to do anything with the rest of my life but sell drugs. *No fuckin' way.* Everything I learned in the program went right out the window. I told myself that everyone I sold drugs to was already on drugs anyway. I just wanted to get my life back to what it was before. Actually, I knew it would be *better* than before.

I got the itch. I wanted to be back on the strip, selling crack, selling cocaine, selling whatever was moving. Like, not *now* but *RIGHT now.* I told Brian that I wanted in, and Brian told me that he'd have to talk to Godfather's son Derrick, who had been an addict for a period but had cleaned up and was back in his spot as a glorified errand boy. Only now he was more of a glorified manager. He still couldn't do much right, but he was the one to go through. As for Brian, he said he was out of the game.

Brian said that he was going to take his money and open up a Quicklie's. I looked at him like he was stupid. That had to be one of the most insane things I had heard in my life up to that point. Quicklie's was a nationwide restaurant chain that served hamburgers, hot dogs, pizza, and ice cream. It even sold breakfast early in the morning, though I had never had breakfast there. I knew that there had been a Quicklie's over by the mall on Jamaica Avenue and one in the big movie theater out by the big mall in Long Island, but I wasn't sure if either one was still there. The pizza sucked, but the hot dogs and hamburgers were good. When I was getting money and used to go shopping on Jamaica Avenue, I would always get the hot dog special: two franks and a medium soda for two dollars and fifty cents. I didn't realize how much I missed eating the food of my choice until Brian brought up Quicklie's.

I missed everything: I missed hot dogs with extra ketchup and shopping in the mall, but most of all I missed the rush that I got when I sold off my inventory and was counting my money. I had never counted off one hundred and sixty thousand dollars, though. I couldn't fathom having that much money in my possession—that would be like someone saying that Earth is 93 million miles from the Sun. There's no way of computing that number in my head. Still, I thought that buying a Quicklie's was the craziest thing I had ever heard in my life.

Within three months, Brian's spot was up and running. He placed the store right in the middle of the strip, next door to the barbershop, where a women's shoe store used to be. There were video games in the back and drug dealers out front. But when customers began to tell the kids not to go in the Quicklie's, Brian started shooing everyone down the block. He was going legit, but he still had a certain aura around him—because he used to hustle and he let us hang around the store, people would look at him like he was still dealing drugs.

That's when I realized that people don't have problems with drug dealers—they have problems with *big* drug dealers. It's like people can be waiting at the bus stop to go to work every day and see drug dealers on the corner. But the second those people are at the bus stop and the drug dealer comes by in a Benz, there's a problem. It's okay as long as he's struggling, but once it seems like he's taking a shortcut, they start hating. When we were all hustling out on the strip, no one said anything. But now that Brian had bought the Quicklie's, we had a base of operations and they hated that. In their eyes, he was still dealing, except now he was a boss. They thought the restaurant was a front and tried to keep people from going there.

At the same time, Brian was pushing us away from the store. He was serious about making it work. He didn't want anything that even smelled illegal going down around his store. No more friends coming in to sell boxes of forks, toaster ovens, and restaurant-issue garbage bags. No more loitering, no more dice games, no more weed smoking. We didn't get it. We were mad. Even I was mad. How the fuck is this nigga gonna tell us to go when he just got the money for the store from doing what we're doing? What the fuck? And he put the store right in the middle of the boulevard, right on the strip that we had been hustling on forever. Hell, be fore the white man came, some Indians were probably selling stuff for their peace pipes right on that spot.

Luckily for me, I wasn't relying strictly on the strip for customers at this time. Derrick had set me up in a house a few blocks over on Rock- away Boulevard. The house was owned by Ray-Ray's father, and he rented four rooms out at seventy-five dollars a week; the two larger rooms up- stairs went for ninety dollars a week. I had a room. Ray-Ray had a room. There was this kid named Markie who originally lived in Harlem but started working in Queens during my vacation. Markie was this slick- talking, fancy Harlem cat who had a joke for every wave in his perfect hair. He had his own room, where he kept all his clothes neatly ironed and cleaned his sneakers with a toothbrush seven days a week. The room where we cooked the coke into crack doubled as a storage area for raw product and guns. We used one room to take girls into when we didn't trust them in our own rooms.

The last room remained empty. But not for long.

"I'm glad they're on our side..."

If anyone aside from Godfather knew their real names, he never told. We just knew them as Grits and Butter, which made sense because they were countrified and inseparable. Where you saw one, you saw the other; and where you saw both, you saw trouble. All anyone could ever really say about Grits and Butter was, "I'm glad they're on our side." And if Grits and Butter weren't on your side, there wasn't much to say about them because you'd never take them for silent killers.

They had come from North Carolina. Actually, they had been *sent out of* North Carolina—not quite chased out, not exactly banished, and not running. Definitely not running, because first and foremost, Grits and Butter ran from nothing. I don't even think those niggas knew how to run. According to them, it was totally their own decision to leave the only home they had ever known to journey north. The multiple life sentences they faced if the authorities picked them up? *Oh, please.* They *chose* not to face those charges, just like they chose to leave three men dead, one paralyzed, one child in a coma, and two women seriously wounded during what was supposed to be a routine cash pickup. The story was that the mayhem was the result of no more than ten bullets, despite the fact that all but one of the victims was running at the time of being shot.

When Godfather introduced Grits and Butter to me, he said that they were there to be enforcers. I couldn't detect anything especially "enforceful" about them. I figured the old man was either keeping tabs on me or practicing more nepotism, like he was doing with Derrick.

Grits and Butter immediately took a liking to Markie because of his slick talk. They looked at his joking like, Markie don't give a fuck about no one. They had never spent much time around kids their own age, so to them there was no such thing as niggas cracking on each other—no "your mama" jokes, no dozens. It's like Grits and Butter weren't raised inasmuch as they were bred for destruction, like the top students in a mercenary-training camp or something.

I didn't realize that Grits and Butter played by different rules until the day I was complaining about this kid Phil. Phil had owed me money for weeks, but I couldn't track him down. Either I had bad luck or Phil had radar, because I would run into people who had *just* been with Phil, who swore he was still just around the corner, who were expecting him any minute, or what have you—but I never ran into Phil. So I said, "When I find this nigga, I'm gonna kill him."

Grits and Butter were checking out the new set of guns Derrick had given them—twin P-Series 9mm Parabellum Rugers, stainless steel with black rubber grips, just like they had asked for. Me, Ray-Ray, and Markie were working in an assembly line: Ray-Ray was bagging the capsules into G-packs; Markie was in charge of stuffing the rocks into vials; and I was the first in line, slicing the coke cookies into pebble-size pieces.

I was complaining about Phil when I cut my thumb with the razor. "Fuckin' Phil," I said. "You see what happens when I think about this motherfucker? I think about this motherfucker and I cut myself. I tell you, I'ma kill this motherfucker when I see him." Now, I'm just talking shit. I meant *kill* figuratively. Plus, I was pissed because I had just chopped off a chunk of my finger. But Grits and Butter just didn't get it. If I had known how they were, I would have said, "Listen guys, I'm a little heated right now. I don't mean for you to go out and shoot Phil." But I didn't know how they were, so I didn't say anything and Phil was shot dead in his chest at point-blank range that night.

The next day, I was telling everyone that I heard Phil got killed. Even though it kind of fucked me up, I was like, Good for his ass. But what really fucked me up was that Markie was laughing when he told me that Grits and Butter killed Phil. That part scared me.

//////,,,,,,,,//////

There are a couple of reasons why Grits and Butter were the way they were, and I came up with them over the years as I tried to understand what made them tick. First off, they were country boys in the big city, and it's well known that country boys hate city slickers. For them, knocking off a city boy or twelve is payback for the way that Northerners look down their noses at them when they come into town in their fancy rental cars to purchase guns and sell drugs. Then there's the fact that they were already guaranteed life behind bars for their North Carolina massacre, and they figured, One life sentence, two life sentences. Is there a difference? That's about all I could come up with. Ten years later, some of the stuff still doesn't make sense. These guys were just *loose*.

In the jungle, combat comes with its own rituals: hissing, roaring, chest beating, marking of territory, all sorts of shit to serve as warnings. For the most part, no wild animal wants to engage in unnecessary mortal combat—it would rather scare off an opponent or escape a predator. It's pretty much the same in the streets. It's only right to let people know what they're getting themselves into, but Grits and Butter lacked this basic courtesy; there was no arguing, no threatening, no facial gestures. For them, everything was pure target.

About a week after Phil's murder, while we were playing spades, Saadiq showed up with his face bloody and swollen. Saadiq was one of Ray-Ray's workers, which meant that he was ultimately under Godfather's protection. Ray-Ray was the type of nigga who switched teams often and had only recently begun to get his own workers, so it was no surprise to see Saadiq come in with his face swollen and fat. "What the fuck happened to you?" asked Markie, but with Markie it came out like a joke, like, "Damned nigga, do you know that your face is fucked up like you fell off the fucked-up face tree, hit every branch on the way down, and then rammed your grille into the trunk for good measure?"

What happened was that Saadiq had found himself in an argument that led to an altercation with Byron and Ricky on the boulevard. Byron and Ricky were brothers, and when two brothers with the slightest bit of thug in them decide to open a can of whup-ass, they're going to reach for the family-sized container. It was evident from the small mountain range on Saadiq's face that Byron and Ricky had scraped out every last ounce of whup-ass possible and smeared it on.

I said, "Shit, nigga, you couldn't even cover your face?" It was a fucked-up thing for me to ask and a fucked-up time for me to ask it, but that was what was on everyone's mind. There was silence for a minute, and then we got into a debate as everyone began to examine his face, trying to figure out what kind of blows he caught to do so much damage.

"That right there look like a right hook."—*"Yo, son, you got a look at the back of your neck? That shit is all fucked up."*—*"Was you on the floor or something, 'cause that mark right there don't look like nothing no fist could have done."*—*"Is your nose broken or just swollen?"*—*"One of them niggas gotta be left-handed, 'cause the way your right side look . . ."*

Saddiq got heated about all the speculation. "These niggas just fucked up my face and y'all lookin' at me like I'm a fuckin' science experiment," he said. I was about to suggest that if he had used some of that anger when he was getting beaten up, then maybe he wouldn't have gotten so fucked up. When he said that we had to go see Byron and Ricky, I realized he was right. We couldn't have anyone fucking with our workers.

We packed up six deep in Ray's mom's hooptie. Grits was driving and Butter rode shotgun. Me, Markie, Ray-Ray, and Saadiq bunched up in the back. When we got to the strip, we saw Byron and Ricky standing next to the bus stop. We were opening the doors and getting out of the ride when Grits told us to hold on. Grits got out of the car and goes over to talk to Byron and Ricky. They were over there talking for maybe about three or four minutes. Byron and Ricky were trying to explain what happened, but Grits was getting pissed. Then Coltrane came across the street and jumped into the situation. Coltrane was one of those big guys who felt like he could just get into shit because he worked out. Grits must've felt like Coltrane was trying to punk him, because he just shot the nigga in the stomach and walked off. Byron and Ricky are like, "Oh, shit," running across the street to Donavan, like, "Help! They shot him." And Donavan's like, "I don't have nothin' to do with this shit." There's action, there's people all over the place, but because no one saw the commotion, no one knew it was Grits. He's just walking across the street like nothing happened.

Grits got back in the car, turned on the indicator, and merged into traffic. "That's how it gets done," Butter said. "One shot, not ten." I was like, What the fuck?!?, but I didn't let on that it was such a big thing to me. And after a while, it wasn't. When Grits got back in, everybody in that car was willing to do what he did, because we knew he wouldn't be asking anything of us that he wasn't willing to do. I started questioning my own heart to see if I had it in me to hit someone as easily as Grits and Butter did. I was still nervous about shooting someone; aside from that time by Tracee's projects, I had never shot anyone—and even that was in self-defense. I was at the point where I could shoot at an inanimate object, like a house or a car, even if people were in it. But just to walk up on someone and shoot him? That was something else.

I just waited for the police to show up. But the police never did, and I began to realize that that's how it gets done. That's when I realized that as long as you don't broadcast your beefs, you get away cold with murder. It's even better if you don't allow the beef to take place. If someone disrespects you, you can know in your head that you're going to get him, but you don't have to show him there's a beef. You just look at it like, Okay, this nigga must not know. And then you fall back and you put it down.

A few weeks later, Ray-Ray came into the house and said that some kids from Rochdale Village had been talking shit to Derrick. This kid Jerome had started mouthing off about the guns his crew had, like, "Y'all niggas got guns? So what? We got guns, too. We got a lot of guns." Derrick had hurt his leg during a game of basketball a few days earlier, otherwise he would have laid on the kids himself. As it was, he sent Ray-Ray to the house to retrieve the guns from downstairs. Ray-Ray was looking for Grits and Butter, but I told him that we didn't need them. This was easy. I grabbed the Mac-11 machine pistol I kept in the house and Ray-Ray took his Tec-9. Then we hopped in the hooptie and drove to the park.

When we got there, I saw a bunch of niggas with baseball bats and two-by-fours. A few niggas had knives and brass-knuckled fists; one guy had a dog chain. I couldn't believe it. I was like, Awww, fuck that. Let me out—I'ma shoot all these motherfuckers just on principle. They were out there like it was the seventies, like we were going to rumble or some shit. That pissed me off more than anything. I jumped out of the car and let off thirty-two rounds at them motherfuckers. I didn't hit shit but air because them niggas got to running as soon as they saw me jump out of the car. Still, they got it in their heads that *that motherfucker don't have no restrictions—he'll air anything out anytime.*

Two days later, I was on the strip when Derrick drove up and told me to hop in the car. He said that this kid Darius was mouthing off at him around the corner. Derrick was going to square off against Darius, but he needed someone to watch his back. When we pulled up, only Darius and Little Stevie were outside. "The rest of them niggas musta went inside," Derrick said. "Just watch Stevie."

Star got out of the car like, Talk that shit now. Darius didn't give a fuck—he just started mouthing off. So everyone squared off: Derrick against Darius, and me against Little Stevie. We were just sizing each other up. I wasn't actively boxing at that point, but niggas knew not to mess with me because I had broken a few noses on the block. I was about to tear into Stevie when Derrick was like, "Man, fuck that! Boo, go get the gun out the car!"

I ran to the hooptie and began looking for a gun but couldn't find anything. I found Jimmy Hoffa's remains, the holy grail, and documentation of alien abductions—but no gun. Darius and Stevie ran up to the house they had been in front of and banged on the door. They were screaming so loud that I thought they had already gotten shot. While I was humped over the bench seat, digging for the pistol, Derrick hopped in, hit the gas, and zoomed off. I was telling Star that I couldn't find the gun when he said that he left because his foot was hurting. I was like, What? Take me home right now. I was heated. There was nothing in the car—he had just been playing games to scare them niggas. He must have had them psyched. He had me psyched.

Later, I realized that Derrick had been using me to scare off Darius and Stevie. It made me feel used, but it also made me feel good. It meant that I was becoming someone to be reckoned with.

IIIIIIIIIIIIIIIIIIIII

We had a crack house on 140th Avenue that wasn't necessarily a crack house but the house of a crack fiend who wanted so many hits so often that she let us take over her crib after she had run out of things to sell. The fiend was cool with the arrangement. She let us push crack out of the spot and do what we had to do as long as we gave her smoke. Her daughter was on some other shit, though, and always talking about, "This my momma house."

The daughter had problems with everything—there were too many people going in and out, we didn't clean up after ourselves. It didn't matter that even before we got there the place was a filthy crack den and anything of value had been sold or smoked away. After all, it was *her momma's house,* and no one could disrespect her in her momma's house. She didn't stop complaining, even after Butter shot her in the leg. Her shit was crazy.

When I got to the crack house, I saw the daughter next to it, clutching her left knee. There was blood in the driveway and a bullet hole in the side of the house. These niggas are inside watching TV. I couldn't believe that shit, like, There's a fuckin' fiend with a fuckin' bullet in her leg in the fuckin' backyard and these niggas are watching TV. I made Markie hose down the driveway while Butter and I dumped off the shot fiend at a hospital in Nassau. But I swear that those niggas would have just left her out there.

Not long after that incident, the house was robbed. Everyone figured it was a setup, because Donavan knocked on the door before some guys came in with guns and caught the place for, like, two thousand dollars' worth of pieces. Grits and Butter took issue with Ray-Ray because he had the gun, so he was supposed to secure the place. But they ultimately held Donavan responsible for knocking on the door. Three nights later, Grits and Butter kidnapped Donavan and drove him to a remote location near City Island in the Bronx. They brought Ray-Ray along and told him that either he shoot Donavan or they were going to shoot him. Ray-Ray shot Donavan point-blank in the head, but somehow Donavan lived. I knew something was changing in me when I felt that Donavan would have been better off dead. The price of life was getting cheaper and cheaper.

///////////////////

After only six months, Brian was unable to meet his payments to the Quicklie franchise and was ordered to remove the sign. The day it came down, there was a little party in the basement of the barbershop—nothing big, just a few heads gathered around. Antoine had just come home from jail on an appeal and his luck was carrying over to the dice. He had won a couple thousand dollars. And then I stole his luck.

I knew from experience that dice was a game of emotion. If I let him get in my head, I'd lose my luck. So I just rolled until I took him for a couple thousand dollars. Then I decided to bank his money. I called over to Derrick and paid up an outstanding debt of seventeen hundred dollars, counting the money right in Antoine's face. Then I paid Brian for negotiations on some parts for my bike, and that was like eight hundred dollars. Antoine got pissed because he felt like he was shooting dice with a little nigga, but the little nigga was busting his ass. He couldn't determine what I was doing with the money that was passing through my hands, but in his eyes, that was *his* money, and now there wasn't much left in my hand for him to win back. When I started playing again, I had less than four hundred dollars to gamble with. I had altered Antoine's whole game. First, I dug deep in his pocket then I left the hole there. New people came around the table and they all started betting money. Antoine got excited, because he saw he could win some money. And for some reason, luck ran from me, right back to him. Antoine started heating up, winning his money back. After about four or five rolls, he was back in the game. His streak ran so hot, he kept winning until I was out of money. When he saw that I was tapped, Antoine held the dice in his hand. "What you still doing here?" he asked me. "You need money to play with the big boys. If you ain't got no money, you can't stand at the table. This ain't a spectator sport."

I couldn't see where this motherfucker got his nerve. So I told Markie to go home and bring back some money that I had stashed in the safe. I also told him to get the money from the room downstairs, which Markie knew really meant, Make sure you bring my Mac—because no one kept any money in the room downstairs.

"I let you bet on air," I told Antoine. "When you was down, your word was good enough. What, my word ain't worth the same hundred dollars?" He looked at me, then at everyone in the room. He knew I was right, so he threw a roll. When the dice landed his way, he stopped the game and waited for me to leave. "Shoot it again," I said.

"Only money talks at this table," he said. "Everything else gotta walk."

Again he looked at me and everyone else in the room. I was heated but I walked away. I met Markie upstairs and came back to the table with the machine gun tucked in my waist. I didn't give a fuck who this nigga *used* to be. The guys in the neighborhood were used to arguing, but I wasn't arguing with anyone anymore. When I was a little nigga, it was okay to play the game like a shorty. I could get mad and show my emotions. But I was getting to the point where I couldn't do that anymore. I was graduating to a higher level of the game, and there was a different vibe. There was no room for running off at the lip. If I ran my mouth off at someone, in that person's mind, I disrespected them and there was a problem. If they were playing the game at the level I was on, then they'd been around long enough to know that if I said I was going to see them about something, I would.

I realized that the people that really mattered didn't say anything. The serious guys knew better than to have any kind of conversation or let anyone know they had any differences with someone. If there was a problem, they'd just tear someone's ass up. And after that person's been shot the fuck up, when they're lying on the floor bleeding, they could figure it out: *Oh shit, maybe I pissed someone off.*

When I got back to the table, Antoine asked me if I had my money. I told him it was coming—he should just shoot the dice.

"Well, you can wait 'til you got your money," he said. "Right now, you gotta step back."

I said, "You know something? When you're right, you're right." I moved back from the table. "As a matter of fact, I don't even feel like gambling no more. But that other money? You ain't gettin' that."

"What?" He threw the dice down and began to come around the table. He figured he'd have to smack someone upside the head in order to reestablish himself after his prison stint, because sometimes niggas won't respect you until you punch someone in the face. He's like, If it has to be a seventeen-year-old punk, so be it. But by the time he got to me, he was staring down the nozzle of a submachine gun. This motherfucker turned white and turned tail. Everyone flew up the stairs because they knew I would do it. And because everyone was running all over the place, I couldn't land a clear shot. I let off four shots, but I hit nothing except the wall.

Mike, the guy who owned the barbershop, came down and sent

me outside. Antoine stayed in the shop, scared to come out. Instead, he sent this guy Chris outside to cop a plea for him. I smacked the shit out of Chris for getting involved in shit that had nothing to do with him. On another day, Chris might not have been the guy to smack, but that day I was heated, so I didn't give a fuck. He came out there talking about, "He did let you shoot on air," and I just smacked his face. I gave Markie the pistol and went in the shop. "You get the fuck out here now!" I yelled at Antoine, before Mike told me to get out of his spot.

Antoine was begging Brian, but Brian stayed out of it. "That little nigga is crazy," he said. "I can't control him." I think that's what *really* scared Antoine, because Brian had always been able to keep me in line. When Brian washed his hands of it, Antoine knew the shit was on. He would not come out of that shop. I sat on the hood of his car, waiting for him to come out until well after midnight. I eventually got tired and went home, but I never did see that boy leave. I think he's still in the barbershop till this day.

////////////////

Some people think that Grits and Butter grew tired of killing New Yorkers and orchestrated the events at Club 100 as their great good-bye. Other people think that the two were just crazy enough to do anything they wanted, and that's why they did what they did that night. Either way, they had reached past the point where anyone could protect them, let alone control them.

The night started out innocently enough. We went to the neighborhood club to soak in the wine, women, and song of a slightly older crowd. It was an older club, but we were able to blend in because everyone knew us. We were all there—me, Ray-Ray, Markie, and Grits and Butter. Everything was cool until we started smoking a blunt in the corner of the club and security told us to put it out.

Markie just kept puffing and blew the smoke into the security guard's face before passing the blunt to Ray-Ray. Ray-Ray started talking shit, because some of the other guys from the projects were smoking on the other side of the club and no one was telling them to put their shit out.

While he was talking shit, Ray-Ray passed the blunt to Grits, who did not understand the security guard, couldn't hear the security guard, or (and this is the one I really think it is) couldn't believe the security guard had the audacity to tell them to put their shit out. "What you say?" Grits asked the security guard, coughing up weed.

"I said, put the fuckin' weed out!"

The security guard said the shit so loud there was no chance of Grits not hearing it. Still, this crazy nigga acted like the message was for someone else. He turned to Butter, "Is he talkin' to me?"

"I ain't sure," said Butter. "I thought he was talkin' to me for a minute there. Maybe he's talkin' to the wall." Butter shrugged his shoulders.

"Must be."

"Must."

These niggas were paying the security guard no mind. Then Ray-Ray started popping shit about discrimination, making it even worse. The security guard got pissed and tried to toss us out, going for Grits and Butter first. They started scrapping in the club, and security was getting the best of Butter. At that point, they took it outside.

Outside the club, the security guard engaged in a round of fisticuffs with Grits while Butter disappeared unnoticed. The security guard made short work of Grits, then with one blow, he sent Markie flying to the ground. Next, he set his sights on me. My boxing instinct kicked in, but watching him make short work of his first two opponents scared me. The security guard was one of those older dudes from back in the day, when a mean knuckle game was everything. I saw no flaws in his technique; I squared up and expected the worst to happen. I was half right.

The security guard looked over my shoulder. His face went blank, like he was seeing the ghost of someone he really didn't like. I turned around and saw Butter running at me, gun first. I moved just in time to escape being shot. The security guard took a slug in the chest and ran across the street. There had been a small crowd out there, but everybody ran when the shooting started. Butter was running behind the security guard with his hand outstretched, his finger squeezing. They zigged and zagged through traffic, and shots filled the air. *Blam! Blam!* With each shot, the security guard's body jerked and changed direction, until he went down on the steps of a junior high school. Then Butter ran over to the security guard and dumped the rest of the clip into him. *Blam! Blam! Blam! Blam! Blam! Blam! Blam! Blam! Blam! Blam! Blam!*

Clik. Clik. Clik.

Out of seventeen slugs, sixteen hit their mark. The next day, Godfather purchased two airplane tickets and sent both of those crazy niggas to Alabama, and Grits and Butter never stepped foot in New York again. But by that time, they had already altered my thought process. Shooting someone was now nothing to me.

*"When it starts to rain,
it really pours on my fucking ass . . ."*

Anyone who hustles hard is supposed to get locked up. He will get locked up—the odds just aren't in his favor. A bona fide hustler doesn't take any days off, which means that he commits a felony three hundred and sixty-five days a year. If you're hustling hard, you'd easily rack up a couple of thousand felonies per year. It only takes one incident to get sent to jail.

The day my odds ran out, I was out early in the morning, getting in some prework drug sales. Train conductors, office workers, teachers—these sorts of people have been known to bypass coffee and doughnuts for a hit of crack cocaine in order to jump-start their day. There's good money in the morning rush hour, so I was out there on a park bench. I had on headphones, and Tricia, this chick I was working with, sat a few feet away on a separate bench. We looked like kids waiting for the bus to go to school.

Some guy I had never seen before walked over to me and asked about copping some heroin. I had been through this once and wasn't going to get caught again. Most fiends aren't going to run up to some random person and ask him for drugs because they don't want everybody knowing they do drugs. They know who does what and they know where to go. So when this guy started asking me about drugs, I told him that I didn't know a thing about drugs or the people who sold them. I told him that I was just waiting for a friend to come by so we could go jogging.

The guy was like, "Well, um, you know, when I come through here I usually see this guy who, um, he's usually here riding a motorcycle." I thought, I ride a motorcycle and I hustle. As a matter of fact, I'm the only one around here who hustles and rides a motorcycle, so if you're talking about me and you don't know you're talking about me even though you're talking to me, then I definitely don't know you. I said, "I don't know what you're talking about."

The guy kept on and asked me if I was "working." I told him to leave me alone and waved him off. Instead of leaving, the guy walked over to Tricia and had the same conversation with her. But he switched it up and said that I had sent him over to her. Tricia didn't know what the guy and I had talked about. She just saw us talking and figured that I had given him clearance, so she sold him twenty-five dollars' worth of crack.

Like five minutes later, three cars of undercover agents came to a stop in front of the benches and placed me under arrest. When they searched Tricia, they found thirty-six vials of crack and twelve packs of heroin in her underwear. "Whose drugs are these?" the cop asked me.

I ignored him, so they continued to ask the stupid type of questions that only cops ask when they're trying to get someone to talk to them. One of them looked at my ID and said, "Curtis Jackson? That's you? Are you Curtis Jackson?" Another looked at my Walkman and asked, "You just out here listening to music? What are you listening to?" The one looking at my ID said, "Where do you live, Curtis?" which made no sense, considering he was looking at my fuckin' ID. Then the one who was interested in my music choices was like, "It's a bit early to be out, Curtis, isn't it?" The guy with the ID went back to the original question: "Whose drugs are these?"

Now, when being arrested by the cops, it's best not to say shit. I should have kept this in mind, but my patience was running thin and I decided to answer the questions as stupidly as they were asking them. When they asked about my name, I was like, "Ain't that what it says?" When they asked if I was listening to music, I said, "Not right now. Right now I'm answering questions." When they noted that it was early, I told them that I wasn't sure because I couldn't see my watch with my hands cuffed behind my back. They asked where I lived, and I said, "In my house." When they asked me who the drugs belonged to, I said, "I don't know. Where'd you find them?"

In the precinct, they got to working on Tricia and told her that I had ratted her out. "You heard what he said when he was asked whose drugs they were," the cops told her. "He said, 'They're hers. Where'd you find them? In her drawers. They're hers.' "

Of course I never said, "They're hers," but after they got to working on her, that's what it turned into. So they told her, "We know these aren't your drugs. All you have to do is tell us whose drugs these are and you won't have to do any time. You'll get off with probation."

////////////

Everything that happens to me happens in spurts. Like when it starts to rain, it really pours on my fucking ass. It never happens over long periods, though. If anyone were to look at my rap sheet, it would look like, God-damn, for these three weeks you were having a really hard time, weren't you? And then there would be a whole long time of nothing, and then it would be like, Damn, it happened right here again. Like one of those heart meters when the person's heart is only beating, like, once a minute, except mine would beat for like three weeks every other year.

Three weeks after the arrest, I was resting in my room with Donna, who was on her way to becoming my girl. It was early in the morn-ing when the door buzzed, which I mistook for the alarm. I reached over, hit the snooze button, and thought about the court appearance I had to make that morning. I figured the court date was just a formality. The state's case against me was nonexistent. I had not been in possession of any ille-gal narcotics. I had not taken part in any conversation that could tie me in with Tricia's arrest. I was caught on tape telling the man to leave me alone. I was not a drug dealer. I had said as much to the grand jury, which I knew was set to conclude that there was not enough evidence to proceed to trial. The district attorney asked me to recount the events of the morning in question, and I told him that I was on a bench, early in the morning, when a strange man appeared and began to ask me questions about my employment status. I said that I wasn't sure as to the man's line of ques-tioning because, at the time, I was wearing headphones and waiting for my workout partner to come meet me. I told the jury that I was an avid boxer who ran three miles around the park in the morning as part of my physical routine. I even had Markie stashed in the hallway, and he was more than willing to come in and corroborate my tale.

The DA just kept asking me the same thing over and over, so I just kept telling him the same thing over and over: "I was just trying to get the man away from me. I don't know where you're from, but where I'm from there are a lot of heroin addicts in the morning. If you have too much conversation with them but don't have what they want, they may hurt you. They seem not to have taken responsibility for their lot in life and react with anger to themselves and the world around them. I'm out there in the morning before I go jogging because I'm a boxer and I run three miles a day most days of the week. Sometimes people will ask me for directions, and when I don't have a clue of where they want to go, instead of not saying anything, I'll say, 'I think it's down there,' because I don't want to have this person in front of me upset. So I'll tell them, 'Down the block' or 'I think it's down this way.' I don't even know why I'm here. If a kid asks me where the store is and I show him the store and he goes in there and buys a beer, that doesn't make me guilty of selling alcohol to a minor. I didn't sell any drugs. I'm caught in this situation for no reason. Let's listen to the tape. You can play the tape and hear the conversation for yourself."

The alarm buzzed again. I smacked the snooze button and prepared to get up when the alarm buzzed a third time. Then I heard the sound of metal slapping against metal coming from downstairs and realized that it was the doorbell, not the alarm that had just been sounding off. There was no mistaking those noises. Only the police would kick in the door so loudly, let alone at eight in the morning. I heard the front lock's cylinder clang onto the floor, and I tried to gather the drugs and paraphernalia that were in the room.

I heard the security gate open and the second, wooden door bang against the wall. The sound of cops' footsteps filled the stairs. I heard them huddled outside my door and knew I didn't even have enough time to split outside the window, much less get rid of the product in the room. Flushing anything down the toilet was not an option. I cussed myself for not having taken the time to have someone rig the room; for a few vials of crack, an accomplished construction worker could have installed piping leading to a stone stash box off the premises. It was one to grow on.

The officers busted in and retrieved a mother lode: two hundred and eighty grams of crack cocaine, four ounces of heroin, cutting agents, vials, Baggies, and more than fifteen thousand dollars in cash, of which only six hundred and ninety-five made its way to the evidence docket. It was a small price to pay considering the twin 9mm Rugers used by Grits and Butter were still in the room downstairs.

///////////////////

I was facing a jail sentence of three to nine years due to criminal posses-sion of a controlled substance with the intent to sell. Denying possession wasn't an option, and the police had followed the letter of the law in my ar-rest. They had obtained a search-and-seizure warrant, executed it, and dis-covered a drug boutique at my residence. The only escape from a lengthy sentence, my attorney told me, was to participate in the New York State Department of Correctional Services' Shock Incarceration Program. The nature of my accused crimes, arrest record, age, and proposed parole eligi-bility made me a prime candidate for participation in the shock program, which would cut my time.

New York started the program in 1987. It combined the best of mil-itary training and the constrictions of jail with the Network approach of substance-abuse therapy—that last part being something I was already familiar with. According to what I had read, shock incarceration was de-signed to establish a proper sense of character while instilling participants with responsibility and correct self-image in order to reintroduce them into society as law-abiding citizens. Certain offenders—mainly those ac-cused of violent crimes and sexual offenses and those deemed escape risks, such as car thieves—were not eligible for consideration in the pro-gram. Shock consisted of a strict physical regimen, substance-abuse train-ing, and extensive academic training. The state looked upon it with favor due to its ability to reduce the skyrocketing operational and capital costs that accompanied longer prison stays. The inmates further impacted the bottom line by performing more than a million hours of community ser-vice per year in the form of clearing woodland, rebuilding communities, and other rural renewal jobs that would otherwise have subtracted tens of millions of dollars from the state's budget. Shock-incarceration partici-pants also boasted better recidivism rates than normal inmates upon release due to AfterShock, the intensive one-year community-parole cal-endar that followed imprisonment.

Most important, it would cut my time from three to nine years down to six months. I was like, Where do I sign?

*"You can send me to jail,
but you're not gonna make me run
through some cold-ass water first. . . ."*

Monterey Shock Incarceration Correctional Facility was located on ten thousand acres of woodland in Beaver Dams, New York, about five hours from the city. There were no razor-wired concrete walls, no sharpshooter-manned gun turrets, no dull gray steel bars—just woods. An unending mess of branches and grass led to the kind of mountains that motherfuck-ers wander into when they are searching for themselves.

The place was staffed by a group of former military drill instruc-tors who felt that the armed forces' short training sessions didn't give them enough time to properly mind fuck people. These bastards took pleasure in rehabilitating the same batch of ingrates day in and day out for six months. To add fuel to their fire, we weren't cadets, we were inmates. If we didn't like shock, it was fairly simple to request a leave and be transported to a real prison to serve out the full jail sentence. But the fact was that the inmates had come to shock in order to escape the longer stays. Shock incarceration was a beast unto itself; the instructors knew nothing but discipline and pain and they had a captive audience to experiment with.

First, inmates were oriented at the Downstate Correctional Facil-ity. Downstate doubled as the processing center for everyone entering and leaving the program. The processing consisted of a two-week session where we underwent psychiatric evaluation and physical examinations to make sure we could deal with what was to come. More than one out of three candidates wouldn't make it through the screening process. Some just weren't physically or mentally conditioned for the regimen; after get-ting an up-close look at what was waiting for them on the other side of the bus ride, others decided they'd rather take their chances in the relatively humane environment of a proper jail.

CHAPTER 15

It was during my orientation period that I met this kid from Brooklyn named Rahmel. Ra was also serving time for various drug charges, none violent. But in actuality, Ra was a stickup kid who was able to toss his burner before he was arrested with a big sack of stolen crack. That gave me an idea, and I told Ra I was going to look him up when we both went home. But first, we had to get through shock.

The woods were crazy. There were no stories of boys who drowned in the lake while running around with hockey masks. But there were lantern-jawed drill instructors who promised that unless you were the best goddamned Boy Scout ever produced by the troops, you'd be lost for longer than the six months you were scheduled to serve if you tried to make a run for it. The drillers also noted that the few inmates who were stupid enough to run were all caught within hours of escaping. They told us that there had been only one incident of disruption among the shock population in the camp's history. Just one. That particular incident took place just four days after the camp's opening and was quickly put down. Ever since then, there hadn't been as much as a fistfight on the grounds.

There was one drill sergeant who was crazy, like he was shell-shocked or whatever the fuck. He had a look in his eyes like he was still in the war. His name was Sergeant Napparan, and he stood all of five feet and two inches. His body was one hundred and forty pounds of pure muscle, and a hundred of it was hanging between his legs. And this motherfucker was in charge of my platoon.

One morning after the 5:30 wake-up, he led the platoon to the camp parking lot for morning calisthenics and drills. It was so cold that I could see the breath come out my mouth and run back inside for heat. Napparan made us drop for push-ups, but one inmate refused. He asked for permission to speak. Napparan walked over to the inmate, leaned back at a forty-five-degree angle to make eye contact, and asked why he wasn't in the push-up position. The inmate was like, It's too cold out here. I'm ready to go to jail. "Sir, the inmate requests a transfer out of the Shock Incarceration Program, sir!"

But the crazy little drill instructor would not let the motherfucker go. He was all up in his face, screaming, talking a lot of shit. Still, the inmate was like, It's too cold out here. I'm ready to go to jail. "Sir, the inmate requests a transfer out of the Shock Incarceration Program, sir!"

Napparan asked the guy what the First General Order was. There were Ten General Orders that we had to memorize; the first was "I will follow all orders given by all staff at all times." This inmate didn't give a fuck about any of that. He just wanted to get dismissed so he could begin his transfer process. It was only ten days into his stay, and he couldn't feel his fingers or toes. He was ready to go to jail. "Sir, it is too cold for the inmate!" he screamed. "The inmate has been issued only one sweatsuit and a pair of canvas sneakers, sir! It is too cold for the inmate! The inmate requests a transfer out of the Shock Incarceration Program, sir!"

After he had a second instructor and security personnel escort the inmate to the filing office, Napparan looked at us and asked, "Is it too cold for the rest of you?"

I spoke up. "Sir, it is cold out here, sir!"

"Cold?" he asked. "This is fuckin' beach weather! If there was a pool, we'd all go skinny-dipping. Drop and give me fifty!" While we were running through our set, Sergeant Napparan removed his sweatshirt and dropped down on his knuckles and began matching us with double-time push-ups, all while cussing us out and telling us to count louder, louder, and louder. He ran through the rest of the morning drill bare-chested.

Before the drill was over, two more people dropped out. By the end of the morning's half-hour run around the grounds, another four had given up. It was like no one wanted to be the first dropout, but after that it was like *whatever.* We had to do a set of fifty push-ups for every inmate who dropped out.

The physical regimen was only one part of the mind-fucking. The other half of the bullshit was made up of the daily meetings, work hours, and academic training. Because I was familiar with that shit from my first rehabilitation experience, it was nothing. And my boxing had geared me up physically, so it was hard for that stuff to get to me as much as the Sergeant would have liked. He really began to hate me and started calling me a "fuckin' slut." But I wasn't about to go to jail—especially not behind Napparan's mind games. No way.

One afternoon we were stumping trees. I was delegated to work the doublehanded saw with this other inmate, Randy Vasquez, who was called a "shitbird." We were the two fuckups—the fuckin' slut and the shitbird. Napparan had figured that making us work together would somehow make us better, but it didn't. While the other inmates hacked at the trees with axes, Randy and I were supposed to stand at attention until the time came when we would finish the job. But I wasn't at attention; I was at ease. To this day, I don't think that there's that much of a fuckin' difference, but that sawed-off drill instructor took his shit real seriously.

Even though Randy was a fuckup, he was the opposite fuckup of myself. For instance, when the platoon was called to attention in the barracks and ordered to sound off, I'd remain silent unless Napparan was right in front of me. Randy, on the other hand, would scream loud and make these crazy exaggerated facial expressions. Everything he did was over-the-top—he marched in double time like he was having a fit, and during exercise drills he hummed the theme to *Rocky* and whispered, "Adrian." So while I was at ease, Randy was standing as stiff as a bar of steel.

I had to do fifty push-ups and then we had to stump the tree. Then we were ordered back to attention to wait for the next tree that needed stumping. When the time came, we were both caught sitting down on logs. Napparan decided that since we liked logs so much, he'd make us carry around logs for the rest of our stays. He said that if we were found doing anything as simple as taking a leak without wood in our hands, we'd be off to jail.

Randy and I carried around those logs for the rest of our stays, though my stay was longer than Randy's. We ate, slept, shit, and worked out with those logs under our arms. My log became such a part of my existence that when I was finally able to move around without it, I felt naked, like a part of me was missing.

////////////////

One morning when the platoon was jogging, Napparan gave the order to march to the left. Marching to the left would have meant the platoon would be running waist deep through a pond. I thought, No fuckin' way. I was a city boy, and running through the water was out of the question. As far as I was concerned, the pond was a swamp filled with lily pads, bugs, alligators, and God knows what else. I continued to march right alongside the road as the platoon ran through the water. I looked over and saw

Randy splashing through the water like a wounded duck. The log was under his right arm and he was sloshing explosions of water into his face. When we got back to the parking lot, Napparan said, "Well, I'll be god-damned! Can anyone tell me what's wrong with this picture?"

Everybody was wet and muddy to their knees except me. It was obvious that one of these kids had been doing his own thing. "Sir! Inmate Jackson isn't wet, sir!" Randy screamed. He was wet to his chest with mud and twigs.

Napparan was in my face. "Inmate Jackson, why the fuck are you not wet?!?"

I bullshitted. I said that with my asthma, my allergy to water, and my fear of drowning, plus the slight cold I had been coming down with . . . as a matter of fact it was the flu . . . The flu had been affecting me. Since the night before, I'd had that scratchy, itching feeling in the back of my throat, which I always had right before I caught the flu. I told Napparan that I must have caught it when I was bitten by an African bee. I said that first the bee bit me, then it stung me. "You should have seen the teeth on it, sir," I said. "That's what gave me my cold—I mean flu. Matter of fact, it could have been a deadly virus. I couldn't risk compromising my immune system by running in the water." This was all understandable, yes, sir?

I was sure that I was going to be shipped off to jail, but I didn't really care. Between the log and the extra sets of push-ups, Napparan seemed intent on breaking me. If he expected me to run through the water just so he could ship me out, he had another thing coming. Fuck it, I thought. You can send me to jail, but you're not gonna make me run through some cold-ass water first.

"You think you're going to get away from me that easily, you fuckin' slut?" Napparan asked. "Lucifer's big brother couldn't get away from me without my consent! You get the fuck out of my face. Report to the infirmary and come back to me when they give you a clean bill of health. I have a special drill designed for you, you fuckin' slut."

The next morning, Napparan took me through the hardest drill ever known to man. I must have done a thousand push-ups, squats, and sit-ups and run the entire length of the country. The drill was so intense that even Randy saw no humor in it. The following morning, I woke up sorer than I had ever been in my life. It felt like every inch of my body had been worked over with a meat tenderizer. I hurt so bad that I probably would have cried if there hadn't been a bunch of people around.

During inspection, I could hardly secure my log. I just rested it on my hip; it felt like the log was holding me up, not the other way around. I looked across to Randy's bunk; he was standing at attention, but his log was on the bed. I looked at him. I wanted to tell him to pick up his log, but I could hardly move. I think I may have shaken my head, but I can't be sure. Even the muscles in my neck felt like they had been set on fire every time I tried to move. Randy just stared back at me. There was no playful exaggeration, nothing. He just looked on blankly. He was through—he was ready to go to jail. I couldn't blame him: He had a one-year sentence, and between the time he had served waiting in Rikers Island and his time at Monterey, he would only have to serve a few months in a regular state prison before he got to go home. He would be in a place where there were no logs and no screaming madmen. I envied him.

From that point on, the only thing I focused on was finishing the shock program and getting out. In a way, Napparan did break me, but there was no way I was going to let him win. I buckled down on my studies and got my GED within a month. Then I started running my old rehab cons during the Network sessions. I did so good that I was even able to lead the platoon for a few days.

Near the end of my time at shock, the platoon was having problems with the monkey drill, which was a big deal because we couldn't graduate unless we did the monkey drill properly. Napparan was like, "What the fuck is the matter with this platoon? All you know how to do are push-ups!"

I said, "Sir, the platoon leader hasn't practiced the monkey drill with the platoon, sir. The platoon doesn't know the monkey drill, and there's no way for the platoon to learn the monkey drill without a platoon leader who can teach them, sir."

"Well, I'll be goddamned, Jackson," he said. "I never thought I'd be saying this, but you're right. For the first time in your miserable life, you're right." He took the leadership baton from the platoon leader and gave it to me. "Jackson, drop that log. You're the new platoon leader."

I knew the monkey drill well because it was a more humane version of the drill that Napparan had given me after I refused to run through the pond. It was mostly for show, just quick movements with extra flourishes that I had no problem with by that time. But not only did I take the platoon through the monkey drill, I also took them through some of the other crazy routines I had been punished with. The only problem was that because of my earlier noncompliance, I had been required to march everywhere in double time, so I had forgotten all the normal cadences. I had the platoon double-time all day, every day: double-time to drill, double-time to the barracks, double-time to lunch. After about three days, the head drill instructor asked Napparan what the fuck was wrong with his platoon. "They're double-timing everywhere like fuckin' morons!"

I told Napparan that I felt the platoon had it easy. "Sir, I think double time is more discipline for the platoon, sir," I lied. "Frankly, I think they're missing the benefits of a truly strenuous workout, sir."

"Don't shit me, you fuckin' slut!" he said. "You don't know any of the other cadences, do you?"

"Sir, now that you mention it, the other cadences do seem to have fallen from my immediate recollection, sir!"

"You fuckin' slut! Give me that baton!"

By that time, we were only a few days from graduation, so I didn't really care. I was on my way home. I was going to be back on the streets; I was far from rehabilitated. If anything, I had become a stronger, meaner, and more focused criminal.

"This is when I started to think big.
Really big . . ."

I had been home for six months. I was still under intensive supervision in the AfterShock program, going to multiple programs and meeting with my parole officer about three days a week. But getting back into the drug game wasn't that hard. After getting up at 5.00 A.M. every day for half a year and constantly working at something, I was conditioned to maximize my time. Between parole visits, I managed to make enough money to purchase a second motorcycle, a brand-new white and blue Suzuki GSX-R750—a speed demon if ever there was one. Then I bought an SUV.

When I arrived at the Toyota dealership I was wearing a dingy white T-shirt with a knapsack on my back, with my headphones on and a bottle of juice in my hand. I was wearing dirty clothes because I had money. It sounds backwards, but I've learned people will treat a person nice when they think that person has a little money. Everyone is willing to do a favor for someone who doesn't need one. When you're riding high, looking good, and you've got some wheels, conversations open up for you. But when you're broke, no one wants anything to do with you. So I saved my good clothes until I needed to project the image that I was doing good. And whenever I actually was doing good, I didn't care too much about my looks, because money talks. When I started to rap, I put it in my music: *I let my whip talk for me, I let my watch talk for me.*

"I wanna get this truck," I told the salesman. I was pointing to a brand-new black Land Cruiser.

The salesman looked at me and said, "Get outta here, kid." He probably worked on commission, and he looked at me as if I were some kid who had just come from summer school. I told him I wanted the truck, and he just looked at me. He didn't say anything for a while.

CHAPTER 16

When he saw that I wasn't going to leave, he said, "I don't have time for games."

I went into the back office where Nick, the manager, was. It was obvious that Nick was running the situation, so I went from the showroom to the door that looked like it belonged to the guy I needed to be talking to. I went back there with my headphones still playing music; I had taken them off my ears but hadn't stopped the tape. I was listening to the Notorious B.I.G.'s *Ready to Die*. I had stopped paying close attention to hip-hop until that album came out. Before that, there was a lot of "punchline" rap going on: "Put a quarter in your ass 'cause you played yourself." That shit was cool, but it wasn't enough to hold my attention. *Ready to Die* changed that. When I was hustling, I would listen to that tape and it would be like Big was sitting right next to me on the bench, kicking what had happened the night before. I could listen to him without losing track of where I was.

There's a part on the album where Big's in this interview and the chick asks him how he started rapping. He was all calm, like, "I just had to get up off the streets." I had never heard anyone talk like that about rapping. He wasn't trying to impress anyone or say he'd loved rapping forever. He was like, It's either this or that. I chose this. I didn't realize it at the time, but that's when I first started thinking about making money from entertainment. Actually, it was the first time I had thought about making money doing something other than selling drugs in ten years, when Sincere put those five Alberts in my hand and my thoughts of throwing parties in the backyard flew out the window.

I was listening to "Everyday Struggle," where Big talks about the Toyota Deal-a-Thon's bargains on trucks. I didn't get in my head that I wanted a truck because I had heard it in a song, but it didn't hurt. I opened up the knapsack and spilled my loot, an avalanche of small bills—singles, fives, tens, twenties—on Nick's desk. "I wanna buy the fuckin' truck."

Nick looked at the mountain of money in front of him. It looked like a lottery win. He screamed out to the guy in the showroom: "What the fuck are you doing?!? The kid says he wanna buy the truck; give him the keys to the fuckin' truck!!!" Nick turned back to me and apologized for the salesman's rudeness. He told me that the guy was his brother by marriage or something like that, and Nick only let the guy work there to keep his wife happy. Nick said his brother-in-law was an asshole to everyone and I shouldn't take it personally. The guy was as smart as he was kind, according to Nick. "This fuckin' guy, he couldn't sell a car for free," Nick said. "But what am I gonna do? My wife, you know?"

Actually, I didn't know. I was a teenager. What the fuck would I know about being married? The whole thing was funny to me. The guy outside thought I was broke and shooed me away. The guy in the back office sees a pile of cash in front of him and he's ready to tell me his life's problems. Nick wanted to know how much money he was looking at. I told him twenty-three hundred dollars.

"That truck is going for twenty-eight," he said. "Six-cylinder, 4.5-liter, 212-horsepower engine; leather trim; dual air bags; antilock brakes; power windows, doors, and mirrors. It has an AM/FM CD player with nine speakers; bike rack on top." He allowed his sales pitch to sink in before he continued. "I'll tell you what I'll do: I'll set up the truck for you. When you bring me the other five thousand, you can take the truck. Under whose name do you want to put the car?"

I said, "Mine."

"Do you have a driver's license?"

"No." My license had been suspended for illegally riding dirt bikes. I used to ride without a helmet, against the flow of traffic, and on the curb, and run red lights—you name it, I did it.

"Okay. Do you have anybody's name you can put the car under?"

"No."

"I'll tell you what I'm gonna do: I'll leave the truck with dealership plates. It has the dealership insurance, but you drive the truck. Any problems, you come to me. When you give me the five thousand dollars, I'll give you the truck."

"Okay."

I drove the truck off the lot five days later and went straight to the Department of Motor Vehicles. I took a written test and got my learner's permit the same day. This was before they had all the fancy computers. I was able to get my permit right over the counter. Then I went to the bicycle shop and had two Gary Fisher mountain bikes loaded onto the bike rack. I never rode the bikes. I just put them up there, sort of like Freedom, who used to have the Jet Skis attached to his 4Runner. Life was good. You couldn't tell me that I wasn't going to deal drugs my whole life.

////////,,,,,,,,//////

A basketball game was held at Drew Park not long after I got the truck. It wasn't any old basketball game, but part of a tournament that attracted top players from all over the country—street-ballers, Pro-Am stars, college players, whoever. The games were an event in Queens and would draw a crowd even though they were played in a different park each time around. The tournament was a big event and I thought it would be a nice marketing move to show up at the game in my new car. I hadn't been driving it long and figured that an eighteen-year-old cruising behind the wheel of a twenty-thousand-dollar SUV would leave an impact, especially at a game where the whole 'hood would be. I had the car looking nasty. It was hot. I had gotten it washed and waxed until it shone like black gold. I went to Canal Street and copped a bunch of new CDs to play from my *AM/FM CD player with nine speakers*. I had the bikes on the roof cleaned down to the spokes—they glistened like sun rays, like my car had four halos on it. I got a bunch of fly little shit for the inside—fresh floor mats, pretty-smelling air freshener—little shit that would give me that extra swagger.

My coming-out-party plan was to show up fashionably late, moving at about fifteen miles an hour to let everyone get a good look at me before I made my grand entrance. I'd hop out, greet the common folk with a shake and a smile, stay the requisite twenty minutes or so that it would take for me to be sufficiently noted, then leave. That was the agenda when I pulled up alongside the park, slowing down to my predetermined fifteen-mile-per-hour limit. Then my plan began to change. The first change came when I saw Roots standing by his cherry red Benz coupe. Roots was only like a year or two older than me and his shine was overshadowing mine. The last time I saw Roots, he was driving an Acura sedan, but he had upgraded, making what I was doing with my Land Cruiser that much less significant. But it wasn't Roots' car that made me rethink my plan—it was the guy next to Roots: a man with dreadlocks, rocking the type of crisp linen that my Uncle Trevor used to wear. But, unlike Uncle Trevor, there was no question in my mind as to whether this guy was a good guy or a bad guy. He leaned on Roots' coupe with a scowl on his face and his hands lay on his waist. A Gucci man-purse was hanging from his wrist. I decided to circle the block while I thought my plan over.

I could have just been overreacting. After all, there wasn't a law saying that a well-dressed, scowl-faced dread could not be a basketball fan. But my instincts told me to think it over. My gut proved right when I got to the corner and saw Terrence's crew on the far side of the park. Terrence's crew was full of guys who had names like Turbulence and Desecrator—not the kind of guys you'd necessarily want problems with. They had real foul auras about them. They weren't even the kind of guys you wanted to hang around with. Like, if you hadn't been dealing with them, then you didn't start. I wouldn't say that Terrence and his crew were friends of mine, but we didn't have any crosses against each other. There was no reason for them not to like me. Still, they were the type of guys who didn't like to see anybody do too good in front of them if they couldn't be part of it. Unfortunately for Roots, he had gotten himself caught up in a squeeze play with Terrence a few weeks before that afternoon.

The whole thing began when Terrence noticed that the younger dealer had copped the new Acura. It was only an Acura, but it was brand-new and Roots was only like twenty years old. Terrence took it on himself to acknowledge Roots' coming up with little communications, like, "What's up?" Just that—"What's up?"—and a pound. Terrence approached the squeeze with patience. He didn't have anyone formally introduce him to Roots because he wanted to make sure that there would be no one to mediate any complications down the line. Terrence was the type who understood that you could skin a sheep only once, but you could shear it year after year. He just pushed his conversation with Roots up the ladder through small talk. "What's up?" became, "What's up, my nigga?" which became, "What's up, my nigga? I see you doin' real good there. Keep shinin'. Show 'em how it's done," which became, "What's up, my nigga? I see you doin' real good there. I need to be on your Christmas list, man. You killin' 'em out there," which became . . .

"What's up, my nigga? Let me talk to you for a second."

At this point, Roots wasn't sure what Terrence had to talk to him about. He was still uneasy with Terrence because Terrence was grimy. But they had been exchanging pleasantries, so in Roots' mind they were cool. Roots didn't have any problems with Terrence, or at least that's what Terrence wanted him to think. Terrence just needed to make conversation in order to get in good with Roots. Roots already knew what type of guy Terrence was and knew he had to show him the respect of a conversation, even if only to get Terrence out of his way.

Terrence was like, "You doin' real good for yourself. I like when I see young cats doin' it. I really like that. I just wanted to let you know that if you ever need anything, I got you. Whatever you need, just let me know. Aight?"

Roots was like, "Aight." He was thinking that it was better to sleep with evil than to run from it. He just ran with it and continued to do the small-talk thing for about a week. Then Terrence motioned him for another private talk.

"You lookin' real good, my nigga," Terrence said. "Listen, I got this thing goin' on in Virginia. I got everything set up, but I just ran a little short for a second. You know, my nigga? I don't gotta tell you—you know how that goes. But I'm a little short for this second, so anything you could do for me, I'd appreciate. I don't ask for nothin' much. I'd appreciate anything you could do for me."

Roots went in his pocket and came up with about two thousand dollars for Terrence. Roots didn't mind the money—two grand was pocket change. If it meant having Terrence in his corner rather than on his back, it was pocket change well spent. But later that week, Terrence and Desecrator cornered Roots by the back of the projects because they had a bone to pick. Terrence was going on about how he had thought Roots was different, that he had thought Roots was someone he could trust, but now that Roots had lent him some money, Roots didn't know anyone anymore. Terrence was claiming that he had shown Roots nothing but love, but Roots returned the love with disrespect.

Roots was genuinely lost. He had no idea what was going on.

"I told you my situation," explained Terrence. "I showed you love, and now you're running from me?"

Roots was still like, "What?"

"How come you ain't say nothing to me when I shouted you out the other day? I was in the truck on Jamaica Avenue and I shouted you out, but you just looked at me and kept going. You disrespected me in front of everybody."

Roots didn't have an answer. And the reason he didn't have an answer was because there had been no shouting out, no truck on Jamaica Avenue, no disrespect. The only thing that there had been was a squeeze, and it was getting tighter on him. Terrence was like, "You think you're better than me 'cause you doing it right now? I've been getting money. You know how I get down. I'm not feeling all that fake shit."

Roots said that he hadn't seen Terrence on the avenue, but Terrence was squeezing it out hard and laying it down thick. He told Roots what he had been wearing and said he had seen him coming out of the sneaker shop and everything. If Roots didn't believe him, he could ask Desecrator, because Desecrator was right there when it went down. Now of course it made no logical sense to have a grimy-ass nigga vouch for the fucked-up word of the first grimy nigga, but what was Roots supposed to say, "Nah, I don't believe you—you're lying." Terrence already knew what kind of heart Roots had. Anyone who's going to give two thousand dollars out of the goodness of his heart to someone he barely knows isn't going to confront a bullshit lie. Roots did the only thing he could: He apologized for a disrespect that never happened. Then Terrence moved in for the kill.

"Like I said last time: I don't wanna ask you for nothin'," he said. "But I just lost fifty thousand dollars. I was telling you about my situation out there in Virginia. I don't wanna ask you for nothin'. But I just need some help getting back on my feet. I'm just trying to get a little change so I can get it rollin' again. I got the whole thing set up. I just need a little seed money. Let me hold ten thousand dollars."

Roots was trying to figure out at what point had they become such great friends that he'd just give Terrence ten thousand dollars. He couldn't say no, because Terrence knew he had it. "I know you ain't got it on you right now," Terrence said. "So I'll check you whenever you got it— on the weekend, whatever. I know you're good for it."

I know all this happened because Roots came and talked to me about it when he realized his predicament. He spoke to a few people about it, but I don't think anyone wanted to get involved. I know I didn't.

As I made my second tour around the perimeter of Drew Park, I saw the scowl-faced dread and realized that Roots was securing up. I saw

Terrence's crew on the opposite end of the park and realized that they were scheming on the scowl-faced dread. I saw trouble and realized I'd be better off at home. There were way too many of the wrong people in the same place. I'd make my grand appearance another day.

It was a good thing, because that night, I learned that the park had gotten shot up. When the first shot went off, the dread was out of there. Terrence's crew knew what he was there for, so they shot him first thing. A clean head shot took him down. They weren't playing any games. After that, everyone in the park who had a gun pulled it out. Before the dread hit the floor, random beefs spilled over because no one knew at the time what direction the shots were coming from or going to. From there, someone would see somebody else shooting in his direction and shoot back.

The park had only one way out—*under* the gate. It was too high to climb, especially with all those bullets going off. Thirteen people had been hit by crossfire; two, killed. It didn't hit me too hard, because the only one who had gotten hit from my side of the 'hood was Ronnie—and he wasn't even involved in the bullshit. Ronnie was just a kid who liked basketball, and he wound up getting shot in the leg. Right now he plays for an NCAA team.

//////////////////////

After the truck, my next major investments went back into my business. I had secured a few solid connections that allowed me to purchase some weight—straight kilos. It was when I started dealing with bricks that I finally understood the economics that Red had kicked to me right before he was killed. *"You don't make money from fiends. You make money from moving product. The more product you move, the more money goes through your hands. The more money goes through your hands, the more money you make. The object is to make as much money as possible go through your hands."*

This is when I started to think big. Really big.

I was going to take the strip. There were a bunch of smaller crews and bullshit little partnerships operating here and there, but there was no real organization. I had been planning it since my return from Monterey and I couldn't believe that no one else had seen how easy it would be. Maybe being away from things allowed me to see them with a fresh eye. Everyone else was too busy doing what they were doing day to day to step out and see the opportunity. Not me. When I came home, I saw it clear as crystal. Everyone who came for drugs came to the strip. They didn't go to the dealer, they went to the spot. Anyone who was in that spot would get the sale as long as the product was available. I had the product; all I had to do was take the spot. And to do that, all I had to do was follow Red's game plan.

I bought thousands of purple tops. I couldn't make a serious move for the strip unless I could put out the biggest capsules available. Most of the kids on the strip were running individual operations, so I reached out to them and told them it would be wiser to work together. There was safety in numbers, and we could all profit by working cooperatively. I was getting work directly from Godfather, and I told them that with one central supplier and a uniform product, we would be able to reduce competition and increase sales. For those who didn't fall in line with my plan, I said that I was offering them the Pablo Escobar plan: silver or lead. You can take money or bullets.

This one kid, Damon, didn't see the wisdom in my approach. One night, Damon approached me on the strip with a handgun. "You're trying to take money out of my daughter's mouth," he said.

"Ain't nobody telling you that your daughter can't eat," I told him. I wasn't scared because I had grown up with him. Damon was a hustler, not a killer. He didn't have the heart to shoot me in public. My reputation had grown to the point that I was able to get enough of the workers on the strip in line with my plan. Damon knew that the other young kids who were with me saw the moves I was making as a way to increase their sales. Because I was buying cocaine in volume, I offered them a greater profit margin than they would have made on their own. Damon knew that going against me meant going against half of the 'hood, and he wasn't built for that. He was just basically showing off so he could say that he didn't roll over easily. I couldn't be mad at Damon; he was just like me. But I was taking over, and that was that.

"I'm not saying you've gotta take packs from me," I said. "I'll give you the raw product on consignment. But if you're going to sell out here, then you're going to get it from me. That's it." Simple as that, he got with the program.

Then I set the second phase of my operation into effect: I called up Rahmel, the cat I met during my orientation into the shock program. That part was simple. I gave Ra all the pertinent information on the neighborhood players—who carried the crack, who counted the money, who held the guns, who to hit first if anybody got out of line. Ra's team took anyone on the strip who wasn't selling purple tops for his work and cash. We had a profit-sharing agreement: Ra could keep the money; I would get the drugs.

Ra's team made it impossible for anyone else to hustle on the strip. Guys who started carrying guns would have to watch out for the cops even more than they already were. What that did was turn them into James Bond hustlers, the kind who worked with beepers and delivered drugs to fiends. Only the most loyal fiends would go through the trouble of calling in for drugs. Buying drugs was an instant-gratification market, and all the extra steps worked against the fiend's experience. Especially after I took the drugs Ra had stolen and let my workers give them away free with the purple tops.

IIII/*IIIIIII*IIII*

Donna had been my girlfriend since the morning I was arrested with the small cache of drugs and paraphernalia in my room, mainly because she stayed in touch. During my six months in shock, she sent me a letter a day. Like every day the chick would write me a letter. I couldn't really think about anything but this chick because I'd receive a letter and then I'd sit down and respond to it. Those letters were the bright spot of my day. When the circumstances had gotten tough enough to make the shitbird opt out for a bona fide prison term, I used her letters to kind of hold me down. I wouldn't say I was in love with the girl, but I came home feeling something enough to let her drive my truck.

It wasn't until I came home from jail that I realized it wasn't a special situation for her to be writing me because she had had a pen pal before me. It wasn't that she was writing because she was that into me. Yeah, she was writing me, but she was already in the habit of writing letters. For her, writing a letter was just a way to pass the time. To her, it was no big deal, nothing special. That isn't why we broke up, though. The reason we broke up involved a double homicide, a police chase, and my dressing up like a woman.

//////,,,,,,,,//////

I was running from the cops. Why wouldn't I have been? I was still on parole, and an arrest for spitting on the sidewalk could have meant that I'd have to finish out a nine-year sentence. I was on my GSX-R750. Even if I hadn't been on parole, I would've been running for the hell of it.

It had started out innocently enough. I was pulled up at a stop sign approaching Guy R. Brewer Boulevard. Because there's a law against riding motorcycles without helmets in New York City, I was wearing a helmet. But because I wanted everyone to see me, it was a half helmet.

Out of nowhere, a squad car passed me, going in the opposite direction. Then the police threw on their sirens and lights and made a screeching U-turn to pull right up alongside me.

"Pull ov—"

I was gone before the words were out of the loudspeaker. There was no way I was hanging around to see what they wanted. Not when I was on my speed demon. Though it had been a long time since I outraced the police, the chase was nothing new. I used to do it a lot when I was younger and riding dirt bikes. The dirt bikes had limited speed, so the trick there was to outmaneuver the cops. The Suzuki wasn't as nimble as a smaller bike, but what it lost in agility, it made up for in power. I used that power to get out of there—and fast. I needed to get out of the squad car's eyesight, so I made the first two right turns I could—straight into Baisley projects. Then I gunned at about a hundred miles an hour for a few blocks before slowing down. I was safe.

It was a quick rush. I marveled at my ability to get away so quickly. I was laughing and making my way back to the strip, when an unmarked police vehicle came baring down on my right at full speed. *Oh shit.* I planted my foot on the asphalt, spun the bike to my left, and took off. *This is going to be fun.* I was excited and intended to make these cops earn their pay before I got off the road and told my story. But any thoughts of recounting the tale took a backseat when I heard the sirens of another police cruiser join the unmarked car behind me. *Now, this is a chase.* Then another unmarked car came roaring from my left, on a perfect collision course. I swerved out of the way in the nick of time. I could feel the heat of its engine on my skin as I ran up the sidewalk. *What the fuck is going on here?!?*

"Turn the fuckin' bike off!" The detective in the passenger seat of the third car was screaming. He was red in the face and close enough for me to hear him over the engines and sirens and screeching tires. "Turn the fuckin' bike off!" he yelled again. "Turn it off! Now!"

Yeah, I thought. *I'ma turn this motherfucker off as soon as I get out of here.*

I was zooming on the sidewalk, but it was slowing me down. I had to remember that I wasn't on a dirt bike. The tricks I used when I was younger weren't an option; I had to get to open road. I jumped back into the street and pulled ahead of the cops. A block up, another unmarked was coming at me, head on. If I kept going straight, the oncoming car could have blocked me off, or worse, slammed into me. I had no choice but to come to a stop. The red-faced undercover that was right behind me pulled onto my left. When he reached out the window for the bike's handlebar, I hit the gas. The bike jerked, wobbled, gained speed, ran up an uneven break in the sidewalk, flew through the air for a few feet, and landed. I was able to break to the left just before the oncoming police car pulled up. Had it been a second slower, it would have clipped my back tire and sent me spinning. I gunned the bike at full throttle and wound up back at the spot where the chase started, going over 120 miles per hour. There was a lot of traffic and it wasn't my light so I made a quick left onto Guy R. Brewer Boulevard. I missed getting hit twice before I fell into the flow of traffic. I wasn't about to look back to see how many police cars were behind me, but I figured there had to be at least five of them. No problem. It was a simple race at this point. No way were they going to catch me. I swerved and dipped, dipped and swerved through the cars ahead of me. There was too much traffic; the police couldn't keep up. It was fun again. When I got to the strip, I popped a wheelie for show. *Ha-ha!*

I had put enough distance between us now. The cop cars were

three-quarters of a block back. It was time to get off the straightaways and onto the back blocks where I could shake them. I jumped the divider and rode against traffic. After a half-block I made a left, turned the bike around, and waited. My adrenaline was pumping. The cops couldn't get to the corner fast enough for me.

When they finally came around the corner, I hit the gas and blew past them in the opposite direction. They were coming on so fast that they nearly crashed into each other when they tried to stop and spin around. *Ha-ha! See you, suckers. I'm gone!*

Zooming down the road, I heard another motorcycle coming up behind me. It sounded like it was inside my head. *Damned, that's got to be a big bike.* Then the ground vibrated and I felt the sound humming in my chest. *No motorcycle could do that.* It was a fuckin' helicopter! *What the fuck is going on here?!?*

I hit Rockaway Boulevard and rode beneath the underpass for a few blocks to get out of the copter's line of sight. When I couldn't hear it in my chest anymore, I turned left onto the North Conduit. I rode against traffic again—if any more squad cars were going to materialize, I wanted to see them coming. I needed to get off the road quick, so I dipped onto 161st Street and zipped into Brian's backyard.

I parked the bike and ran. It wasn't the time to figure out what was going on. Once I was hidden I could stop and think. For the moment, the only thing on my mind was running. I sprinted back to my grandmother's and snuck in through the window like I used to as a kid. No one in the house saw me and I hid in the attic.

I may have only been up there for a few minutes, but it felt I heard a police cruiser pull up in front of my grandmother's house. It was a police cruiser, no doubt—I could tell by the way the car came to a stop and the doors slammed, even before I heard the cop's knuckles knocking on the front door.

From the attic, I could hear the cops—one White, one Black—speaking to my grandmother. Officer White was explaining that Curtis Jackson was a suspect in a double homicide: two young girls had been murdered the night before and the suspect fled on a white and blue Suzuki GSX-R750. *Wait a minute—I'm Curtis Jackson. What the fuck?*

I heard my grandmother gasp and drop onto the couch. Then my grandfather came in, wanting to know what in the hell two officers were doing in his house.

Officer White recounted the story: two murdered young women, one white and blue Suzuki GSX-R750. Suspect Jackson had just led five mobile units on a high-speed chase through the neighborhood. They knew it was Jackson because his half helmet showed his face. One of the pursuing officers had gotten close enough to put his hand on the bike, but the suspect eluded him. Any assistance the Jacksons could provide the investigating officers would be appreciated.

"You can assist yourselves right out my fuckin' door," my grandfather said.

"Sir, I understand you're upset," said Officer White. "But this is a criminal investigation of a homicide. If you're harboring your grandson, you can be charged with obstructing justice."

"Hell, I'm upset 'cause you're in my goddamned house," Granddad said. "And if you don't assist yourself out my house, you'll be harboring an obstruction right up your—"

Yeah, Grandpa! Tell 'em! It was a crazy moment. I was proud of my grandfather for having my back. Over the years he had always been on his own shit and kinda distant from me, but right then and there I knew he loved me. At the same time, my grandmother, the closest person in the world to me, is going crazy. And then there are the cops, saying that I'm wanted for murder.

"Sir, your grandson is a criminal suspect in a homicide," said Officer White.

"Well," my grandfather said, "if you stay in my house one more damned minute, he won't be the only one."

"I can take care of this," Officer Black said to Officer White. "Let me take care of him."

"What?" My grandfather was on his shit for real now. "Let *you* take care of *me*? In *my* house? No, I'll take care of you! Get out!"

"Sir—"

"Get out!!! Don't be coming to my house talking about you're gonna take care of me. I'll take care of *you*. Shit, I can take care of eight of you." My grandfather cussed them right out of the house.

On the porch, Officer White asked Granddad about Suspect

Jackson's motorcycle. My grandfather asked whether it was illegal for a black man to have a motorcycle. They saw my Hurricane and asked about that bike like, "These bikes are very expensive."

My grandfather was like, "If he could have one bike, then he could have two. Hell, I'll buy him a dozen motorcycles!" he yelled. "You comin' to my house like he's guilty because he has a motorcycle. You're full of shit."

"Sir, if your grandson isn't guilty, why did he run?"

"Hell, I'd run from you, too. You kill everyone you catch!"

I was like, *Yeah!* I would have shouted it out loud if it weren't for the fact that it would have landed me in jail. When the cops left, I knew two things for sure. One was that I had not killed any two girls the night before. The other was that the current model Suzuki GSX-R750 came in two color schemes: white with blue, and white with orange, so the only thing for sure about the murder suspect was that he had good taste in motorcycles.

I snuck into my grandmother's room and grabbed a wig, a sundress, and a few dollars in quarters. I put on the disguise and walked to Rockaway Boulevard where I grabbed a cab to the mall in Long Island. I was in the back of the cab, taking off the dress, when I saw my black Land Cruiser drive past, going in the other direction. Donna was driving, and some guy I had never seen before was in the passenger seat. If it hadn't been for the cops on my ass, I would have made the cab turn around and chase down the car. But I was on the run.

The first thing I did at the mall was call my parole officer: "Remember I told you I was gonna buy a bike?" I asked. "Well I got it. I got it and I washed it and I rode it down the block. As I was waiting at the corner, I saw the police flashing their lights at the other end of the block. So I went in and put the bike in the driveway. Later, the police came by my house and said that they were looking for me as a suspect in a homicide. They said the guy had a bike that looked like mine."

"Where are you at now?" she asked.

"Out."

"Out? That doesn't help. You're not gonna dump this shit on me, Curtis. I'm not here to pick up after you." I didn't say anything, and then she asked, "Is there anything else I need to know?"

"No. That's it. I didn't kill nobody."

"Okay. I'll see what's going on. Do you have a number where I can call you back?"

"That's okay. I'll call you." I hung up and called Donna. Between Donna's mom's work schedule and her sister's college courses, the one car the family had was not enough for everyone. So on Mondays and Wednesdays, I would let her drive my car to school. My one condition was that she let no one else in the car. I told the bitch, "Don't have nobody in my car."

"Did you have someone in my car today?"

"Uh, yeah. I, um, I gave Sharise a ride to pick up her son from day care."

I had known Sharise since she couldn't cross the street. Actually, it was Sharise who had introduced me to Donna. I didn't recall seeing Sharise in the car, but I hadn't been able to see fully inside. So I probed further: "You had anyone else in there?"

"Nah . . . oh, yeah. I gave my friend Victor a ride to the bus stop."

"Victor? Who the fuck is Victor?"

"He's a friend from psychology class. I told you about him."

"No, you didn't, bitch."

"What?"

"Bitch, I told you not to have nobody in my fuckin' car."

"I was just giving him a ride to the bus stop."

"So you put the 'friend' from psychology class that's just going to the bus stop in the front and have the chick you known all your life in the backseat?" She didn't say anything, so I said, "You take all the shit I bought you: all the jewelry, the clothes, the shoes—"

"No. I had her in the backseat because . . . because she wanted to be with Mario. You know he's only three, and she didn't want him all alone—"

I ignored her and kept going. "As a matter of fact, you can keep the shoes and the clothes. Just give me my clothes that I left over there. And them earrings and that chain I got you, the purses, all that shit; put it in the car and I'ma come to pick it up later."

Donna began to cry. "Why are you doing this to me?"

"Bitch, I told you not to have no one in my car."

"I'm sorry," she cried. "I won't do it again."

"I know you won't, bitch. I'm coming to get my shit."

"How can you be so mean?"

I hung up the phone. That was it for me and chicks. Either I had bad luck or they were just no good. I was through with taking them seriously. Besides, I had bigger fish to fry. I called my parole officer again.

"I spoke to the detective handling the investigation," she said. "They made some sort of mistake. They know who they're looking for now. But they want to know why you ran. I'm not going to ask you if you had anything on you that you shouldn't have had, but that's what they think."

"All I know is I can go to jail if I make police contact," I said. "They came at me, but I didn't know what the fuck they wanted. So I ran."

"I get it," she said. "I deal with this all day. But tell me something: How long have you had that bike?"

"Like two weeks," I lied. "Why?"

"Well, they claim you were going 160 miles an hour through red lights, making all types of turns, popping wheelies, and gunning against traffic."

"Me?"

"I don't want to know," she said. "But I expect you to take the bus to our next meeting. They confiscated your other bike, and I don't think they'll be too happy to see you riding your Suzuki anytime soon."

"My other bike?"

"Yeah. You know, the Kawasaki you never told me about?"

"Oh, that one."

"Uh-huh. Yeah, that one. That's how they know it wasn't you. They lifted the prints off of it. They're holding it down at the precinct for you. Do you want the number? They'd love to see you."

"No, that's okay. I'll find another way to get around."

"That's what I thought."

I took a cab to Donna's house and picked up my truck. When I got home, my grandmother told me that the police had been looking for me. I told her that it was a case of mistaken identity, but she didn't believe me until I put her in touch with my parole officer. Although I had been making moves since I had come out of shock, she wasn't aware of my dealings. She knew that my intensive parole kept me out of the house most of the time, and I never parked my SUV on the block for her to know about it.

At some point during the chase, I somehow managed to peel the skin off my right forearm. It was dripping with blood, but in all the excitement I didn't even notice the wound until my grandmother pointed it out to me. I told her that I had fallen off my motorcycle, which was close to the truth. She took me into the bathroom, cleaned off the wound, and applied some dressing. "I pray that you're not getting back into trouble again," she said. "You can only get so many chances before all the bad that you do catches up with you."

I lied and told her that I was keeping my nose clean, but I knew she was right. Sooner or later, things would catch up with me. And I didn't want to keep on lying to her. That part bothered my conscience more than selling drugs.

////*////*/*/*/*/*////////

Even though I was nearly in total control of the strip, I began to walk more often. One day, I was walking down the street not far from my house when I saw a black Land Cruiser, almost identical to my own but with extra-dark tints on the windows, parked on one of the side streets. I made no more note of the car other than it was damned-near a twin of my own and continued on my way.

"Psst! Psst!" A set of lips called to me from nowhere. Then I heard the whisper of a voice I hadn't heard in years: "Yo, Boo-Boo, man. C'mere."

When the window of the parked truck slid down, I saw Sincere resting behind the wheel. "You seen that lawyer chick, man?" he asked before I was fully in the car. His eyes shot up and down the block.

"Lawyer chick? What lawyer chick?"

He looked over his shoulder, checked his rearview mirror, then motioned to a small spot on the corner that was a notary public, real-estate broker, accounting firm, and, copying and faxing service, all in one. "Nah, I ain't see her today," I said, even though I wasn't sure who worked in the store. I could have just passed the woman on the street and not known who she was. I was surprised to see Sincere: He had been arrested on a minor charge that landed him in Rikers Island for eighteen months. When he came home from his bid, I was in shock. When I came home, Sincere had disappeared. But word had it that Sincere had just come back to town with almost a million dollars in cash. The money made him a target. In fact, Turbulence, Desecrator, and a few other unsavory types had designs on catching him for his loot. Derrick had even approached me with an offer to orchestrate a robbery with Rahmel for 10 percent of the take. I turned down the offer, not out of loyalty to Sincere, but because Derrick's plan consisted of kidnapping Sincere's sister and grandfather for ransom. I played stupid for a second to gather some information. "What's going on?" I asked.

Sincere explained that things were going down the drain quickly. He said it all started when he brought Coltrane to Alabama with him—Mobile, to be exact. And Mobile was the place to be, because two interstates ran through the town. "You got I-65 running north and south and I-10 running east to west," Sincere explained. "So you've got a lot of drug traffic coming through: west from Texas, Louisiana, Mississippi; east from Georgia; north from Nashville and Kentucky; and, best of all, man, from the South—Florida, man, Cubans, Dominicans, Haitians. It's like the fuckin' crossroads of cocaine."

Sincere had taken Coltrane down because he needed a few good men to run his operation. Problem was Grits and Butter—*those fuckin' crazy-ass niggas*—were down there, too. Same town, Mobile, Alabama. Now, Mobile, Alabama, ain't but so big and it was only a matter of time before they crossed paths with Coltrane. The craziest thing was that Grits had not even recognized that Coltrane was someone he had shot at a bus stop on Guy R. Brewer Boulevard just a few years prior. But Coltrane got scared, becoming real uneasy every time he saw those crazy-ass niggas. He began sweating and stuttering and shit. After a few weeks, Grits and Butter got picked up by the police for shooting a security guard in New York.

It was clear to everyone that Coltrane had snitched on Grits and Butter. Less than a month after those crazy-ass niggas were arrested, the police began shutting down all the drug businesses in Mobile. Not just the police, either, but the feds—the FBI. Sincere put his money in a bag and drove back to New York with Coltrane, but the feds were putting together a serious case. Now they were after Sincere and Coltrane. Shawn had been down to Alabama and he got picked up. Brian had been down to Alabama once or twice, so he was probably being investigated. A lot of other dealers from Queens were being looked into. The more dealers who fell, the bigger the federal investigation grew. "Man, these niggas is tellin'," Sincere said. "I don't even know why they gotta be like bitch-ass niggas. Man, I'm not goin' to see nobody. They gotta come see me."

Sincere said he had a plan. He had seven hundred thousand dollars in cash in the storage compartment of the truck. "I'm buying houses, man," he said. His plan was to buy six houses and have third parties sign the deeds. He knew that the feds would catch up to him eventually, but before that, he'd put his money into real estate and save some for his appeal. When he came home in a few years, he'd have houses to sell. "I'm not gonna do no stupid shit like Brian did and buy a restaurant, man," he laughed. "I'm about houses and shit. Real estate is the way. No upkeep, no overhead. I'ma buy these houses and sit on 'em 'til they worth a lot of money. Did you know that a huge percentage of the wealth generated in this country comes from real-estate investment? I'm looking at Donald Trump, not Chef Boyardee."

But he had to be careful. Coltrane had run his mouth to the wrong people about Sincere's money. He heard that people were trying to kill him for his "little bit of money," so he took it with him everywhere he went. I tried to find out where he was staying, but all Sincere would say was that he'd be right next to his money.

More and more, I began to realize that the drug game wasn't stable. I knew I had to have something to do with the money once I accumulated enough to leave the game behind. The last thing I wanted was to be on the run with a duffel bag full of cash.

////////,,,,,,,,////

I decided that it was time to get the Mercedes-Benz that I had always wanted. Not only was I making a bit of money from my control of the strip, but I had a man wanted by the Federal Bureau of Investigation and every stickup kid with a gun riding around in the same model car as mine. After my motorcycle chase, I wasn't thrilled about having another mistaken-identity crisis.

Donnie, this young kid dealer from South Jamaica, told me about a car dealership in Baltimore that dealt in cash and asked no questions. Donnie also told me that business was brisker and the price for raw coke was much higher in Baltimore than in New York, so there was a greater profit margin. I decided that bringing along an eighth of product would more than pay for gas money.

My first day in town, I went to the dealership and negotiated to trade in my Land Cruiser for a S430 Mercedes sedan. The dealer told me it would take a few days to run the paperwork and inspect the trade-in. Then I went to see Donnie to pass the time.

He was working out of a spot about a half hour from D.C. Some thing struck me about the operation as strange. The whole business was executed from one apartment—manufacturing, packaging, distribution, and resale. It didn't feel safe; the place seemed like a trap. Donnie explained that the police didn't come through a lot and usually made a lot of noise when they did. There was a man in an apartment upstairs who kept lookout from his window and would alert them in enough time to get out through the back window. The product would have to be lost, but they'd escape arrest.

"What if there are cops by the back?" I asked.

"If there are cops by the back, then you're fucked," Donnie said. "But the guy looks out the back window, too."

It was a risky operation to say the least, but the volume was just as Donnie had said. I was able to knock off half of the eighth before my car was ready. In another four days, the other two ounces were done. The eighth had cost me twenty-three hundred dollars in New York; cooked and pieced out in Baltimore, it sold for about eight thousand. After paying for use of the space, I pocketed over four thousand dollars.

Four grand for a week's work was a good deal, but staying in one place until it was time to go to jail didn't strike me as a viable business model. I came up with a solution: I gave Donnie a quarter kilo of cocaine on consignment. He would cover the rental fees and handle the manufacturing and resale. In two weeks, I'd come back for a payment of twelve thousand dollars, at which time I'd give him a free eighth of raw product. "So it's like for every two eighths you pump for me, you get one free."

It was a short-lived arrangement, however. After securing his first bonus eighth, Donnie was arrested when undercover narcotics agents burst into the apartment through the back window. It sounded too good to be true, and it was. It seemed more and more that the game was closing in on me, but not enough for me to stop. I knew the odds going in, and I still thought that I could beat them.

*"She would become the mother
of my first son . . ."*

I had noticed her a few months before, when I was still involved with Donna. But that wasn't what stopped me from pursuing her. She said that she was involved in a relationship. But that didn't stop me, either. What stopped me was the way she told me, in no uncertain terms, that she was a student of loyalty, respect, and fidelity—if not to the person she was seeing, then definitely to herself. So what stopped me was the *way* she said no.

She was on her way to school, waiting at a bus stop. I still had my Land Crusier when I first met her, but I hopped out and walked over to where she was sitting. Something told me that she wasn't the type of girl to take seriously a nigga tossing random lines at her from behind a steering wheel. I introduced myself, and asked if we could exchange numbers to set up a date. She said, "No."

I said, "You mean not now."

"If that's what you need to hear in order to feel better about yourself, fine," she said. "But I'm saying no."

"Well, *no* only means 'not now.' "

"I'm answering you in the time you're asking me," she said. "You're asking me right now and right now I'm saying no."

"So . . . you're really just saying 'some other time.' "

"No. I'm saying no."

"Isn't that like a double negative or something?" I asked. "I think that means you're saying yes."

She smiled, shook her head, and said, "You're not going to give up, are you?"

"Oh, no," I said, moving closer to her on the bus-stop bench. "Not now." I was intrigued and impressed by her. I couldn't articulate what was so different about her. I knew that she would never respect me if I didn't respect her decision and her relationship. I said, *"No* is so final." It's a word that means forever and never, and even if in my world it means "not now," I was no longer in my world, but in hers, and I'd stay there as long as it took for the bus to come, because when it came, it would mean that I'd have to go back to my world, where *not now* means *forever* and I'd never see her again.

She laughed and said that I was either a player or a psychologist, but she couldn't tell which for sure. I said that I was just a guy who was visiting her world, and she said that I definitely was a player and that she was no queen of any world, but just a girl at the bus stop who was running late for class. I said that she had to be majoring in something that didn't involve English because of her use of a double negative. Then she said that she had been wrong; I was neither a player nor a psychologist—I was a comedian. She told me that she was a business major and wanted to own a string of beauty salons, though she'd be content to start with just one in the neighborhood. By the time her bus arrived, we had discussed higher education, psychology, business, and comedy. I thought it was a good start.

As she got on her bus, I said that I had enjoyed our conversation and would be returning to my world, where *no* means "not now," and if the laws that govern her world ever change and the properties of forever or never become less final and more negotiable, I'd be glad to pay her a visit. She said that she had never said "never," she had only said no, which means no, as in "no," not no as in "not now." And she got on her bus.

Her name was Tanisha, and she would become the mother of my first son. Did I know it that day at the bus stop? I don't know. But I knew something.

The next time I saw her was at a pizza shop on Jamaica Avenue. She was with her friends, and I felt her staring at me before I got out of the black Mercedes and ordered two slices. I stared back without being able to place her at first. When I figured out who she was, I asked her if the answer was still no. She questioned my bluntness but said that, no, the answer wasn't no and that if I could figure past the triple negative, it would only mean that she would take my number and nothing else.

////////////////

Well, I got her number and a whole lot else. A few months later, she was pregnant and we were already arguing all the time. One time, I was walking down the boulevard with Ray-Ray's girlfriend, who was telling me some funny shit that Ray-Ray did. I had my arm around her, getting all the dirt and laughing when Tanisha hops out of a dollar van and gets in my face. "Who the fuck is this bitch?" she asked.

If she hadn't been pregnant, I would have hit her so hard she wouldn't have known what day it was. I spent all my time making niggas show me respect in that environment, and she chooses to grandstand on me where I work. I'm like, This is my workplace; you on the strip right now and you come out here with that bullshit. She got away with that one but I told her, "You were wrong. If I seen you talking to somebody, I wouldn't act like that."

That was the biggest argument that took place between us up until that point. She was jealous about the girl, and that was an argument I could have won hands down. But she was also beginning to get worried about my lifestyle, and that wasn't as easily dealt with. She said that what I was doing was cool when I was just her boyfriend, but I was about to be the father of her child. She was worried about the example I would set for our baby. That made me think. I knew I had made my own decisions and maybe I didn't always make the right choice, but I wanted my child to have more options than I had. I mean, I was hustling so that I wouldn't have to hustle anymore. I sure as hell didn't want my kid growing up thinking that hustling was the thing to do. I didn't want to be one of those parents on the "do as I say, not as I do" tip. I knew all too well how alluring the drug game could be. I know that one of the reasons I had fallen into it so easily was because I watched my mother do it. *Mommy does it, so it can't be that bad.*

Tanisha really made me think long and hard about myself. She said that she didn't like the idea of having to raise a kid by herself if I wound up in jail, or worse. That's when I started to think about doing something besides selling drugs. I had a kid coming and I didn't want to raise my son or daughter in that world. And more important, I wanted to be there to be part of my child's life.

*"I was on my way to
being a rap star . . ."*

A few months later, I met Jam Master Jay. It wasn't planned or anything, it just happened. I had gone to a nightclub in the city and some mutual friends introduced us. He liked my style and I told him that I wanted to be a rapper. I was half kidding, but he liked my style. He saw that I was a young kid rolling in a Benz and that I had some money. He also knew that I was from Queens, and the guys who introduced us told him what I was about. He saw me as a kid who was trying to get out of the game, and he respected that. Jay was a good guy like that, so he said he'd put me on. I thought he was just bullshitting me. This was Jam Master Jay from Run-D.M.C.—they were like the Beatles of hip-hop. They were pioneers and legends. I figured there was no way that Jay would work with me, but the next day I went by his studio and he gave me a CD with a beat on it. He told me to write to it and come back to him when I was done.

I didn't know what I was doing. I had never written a rhyme. But I looked at it like it was my chance to get out of the drug game, so I hopped on it. I wrote to the CD, rapping from the time the beat started to the time the beat ended. I went back to Jay's studio a few days later and played him what I had done. When he heard it, he started laughing. He liked the rhyme, but he said that he had to teach me song format—how to count bars, build verses, everything. On the CD I had given him, I was just rambling, talking about all kinds of shit. There was no structure, no concept, nothing. But the talent was there. He said that he'd sign me to his production company. At the time, he had a label deal through Def Jam and had already scored big with Onyx, a group of guys from my neighborhood who had already sold millions of records and were about to start work on their third album. I didn't even look at what I was signing—I was on my way to being a rap star.

I didn't know about the music industry, and I thought, I'm on. As I saw it, it wouldn't be long before I was making videos and some legal cash. I turned my back on dealing drugs and focused on music. Some kids I knew from Rochdale Village, Jamal and Roger, had turntables up in their crib. I began to hang with them and make freestyle tapes just for fun. At first, we would just rap over instrumentals and say whatever. But I started preparing myself and thinking about what I was going to say to beats. I was cheating because we were supposed to be freestyling, but I ended up writing my shit. My stuff came out better than theirs because I had thought my shit out. I had fun with it. Because of rappers like the Notorious B.I.G., Tupac, and Snoop Dogg—all had sold millions of records talking about the streets—I didn't feel like I had to compromise who I was to make music. I wrote about the things I had seen in my life and what was going on in the 'hood. I was able to express myself better in rhyme than I ever had in a regular conversation. Not only was it fun, but I was going to be able to get paid for doing it. I couldn't beat that. For the first time in my life, everything was falling into place. I felt like I finally knew what I was supposed to be doing with myself.

In school, you're supposed to figure out what you're good at and then you go do that for a living. I never learned in school, but when I found music, I found my direction. That's when I really realized what I wanted to do, what I was good at. No one could tell me anything else. Everyone thought I was crazy when I told them I was going to start rapping. Everybody in the neighborhood who had been hustling for me was looking at me like I had fallen and bumped my head, but I couldn't have cared less. I knew what I was doing and where I was going. *The next time you see me, I'm going to be on TV.*

I came up with the name 50 Cent because I thought it was catchy. I'd already thought of the whole concept as a metaphor for change, and I decided, I'm going to change the game. That was how I felt. I knew that no one was talking about the stuff I was talking about in the way that I was. By that time, Biggie and Pac had been murdered and the other guys who inspired me had moved on to talking about their fame and riches. I was still talking about the street life. And I wasn't just talking about it in general, I was talking about real-life situations and real people who were heavy in the game. I knew my approach was different.

I wasn't going to run with the attitude of telling people that I had actually taken the name from the *real* 50 Cent. I just felt it was something an insider would get and the rest of the world would just think it was catchy. The *real* 50 Cent was a stickup kid from Brooklyn who used to rob rappers. He had passed, but he was respected on the streets, so I wanted to keep his name alive. Other rappers were running around, calling themselves Al Capone and John Gotti and Pablo Escobar. If I was going to take a gangster's name, then I wanted it at least to be that of someone who would say "What's up" to me on the street if we ever crossed paths. I couldn't see Gotti or Escobar giving me the time of day.

There were a lot of other street gangster names I could have taken, and some rappers after me took some of the names I passed on. I liked "50 Cent" because it seemed like something that people would remember—even a little kid is going to remember "50 Cent," especially when he starts to learn how to count money. I figured if they're old enough to recite words, then they're old enough to remember the name 50 Cent. I felt it was broad enough to lend itself to other things.

I began to market myself as 50 Cent. I bought a gold chain that had a quarter and five nickels arranged like a cross. I made a sticker of a fifty-cent coin with my face on it and the phrase "In God We Trust." I didn't even think about dealing drugs because Jay made me promise to leave all of that alone. He said he didn't want that type of energy around him and wouldn't work with me if I was still in the streets. The reason he had taken me under his wing was to give me an out from what I was doing. I respected where he was coming from. I didn't get into the drug game because I thought it was a cool thing to do. I got into it to make money and I didn't see any alternatives. If rapping was going to get me out of the 'hood, so be it. Just give me the beat and put me in the studio.

But then I got my first education in the music business. I had been signed to Jay for months, but my riches were not coming in. There were no finances involved in the Jam Master Jay deal—he let me use the studio, but I didn't have a record deal. Before that, I didn't even realize there was a difference. I thought that signing to Jay meant that I was *on,* but it just meant that I was waiting in the wings. Because I had stopped working in the streets, I wound up selling off my car and a lot of my jewelry in order to provide for myself. I had my lifestyle already, which I had become accustomed to. But I had to let that go. I was adjusting to not having things and not being out there on the strip. I was writing music all the time. Instead of selling drugs, I was in front of a boom box all day, trying to write raps to everything that came on. I was too close to making it to turn back.

//////,,,,,,,//////

My rap career took longer to jump off than I thought it would. I was making songs like "Somehow the Rap Game Reminds Me of the Crack Game." And I was sitting there watching my songs come out on a Jay-Z album. I did that song before Jay-Z came out with his, but when I played my version, people were like, "He's trying to be like Jay-Z." I was like, "Get the fuck out of here. This is my life." I felt like Jam Master Jay played my record around the wrong people. In my mind, I began to think, I need to get away from this nigga. He's supposed to be helping me, but it seems like he's really holding me back.

I learned how to do songs and that's all I really needed. I remember making this one song called "The Hit." I was psyched because everybody was feeling the song and no one was saying that it sounded like Jay-Z or some dumb shit. But then Jam Master Jay said something to me that blew my high. He said, "Yeah, that shit is hot, but make another one." It fucked me up because I felt he was being sarcastic. I wasn't really feeling that shit, but I realized it was real. I had to see that no matter how hot a record is, *make another one, nigga.* I *had* to. While that one was hot, I had to be somewhere making another one to follow it up, or I'd be finished. "You're only as hot as your last hit." I carried that with me. The first time I heard a nigga say it to me, I didn't like it, but that's the reality of it. That's the way things are. I still had a lot to learn about the music business.

After being broke for a few months, Jam Master Jay got me on a song called "React," the third single from Onyx's *Shut 'Em Down.* At the time we did the song, no one expected it to be a single. They just put me on the song as a favor to Jay because I was the new nigga in his camp. But radio DJ Funkmaster Flex was feeling it, so they shot a video for it. The video concept called for us to be hockey players. I thought it was a stupid-ass idea. It may have been a good idea to try to cross over and get the white folks' attention, but it was difficult because you had fifteen niggas busting their asses, trying to learn how to ice-skate.

The song and album didn't take off, and I was at the end of my rope. Jay may have taught me how to rhyme, but the situation wasn't working for me on the whole. I still wasn't getting the main thing I was in it for: money. The bottom line is that, at the end of the day, it's about dollars and cents. Jay was a cool nigga, but there was no money coming my way. What does it matter how cool he was when I had to feed my family?

////hₙₙₙₙₙ////

Things were going bad between Tanisha and me. I can't help but think that it was because I had no money. We had other problems, but when you're broke, money seems to be the answer to everything. I thought that if I had some income, then we would be able to smooth things over. But there was no cash and we were always beefing. Things seemed to be a lot cooler when I was working and could buy her stuff. When I met her, she was the ideal person I wanted to be with: She was staying by herself, above her mom's barbershop; she was in college; and she had a job. She was the opposite of me, since I didn't have my own place at the time and I was selling drugs.

While she was pregnant, she had nice clothes because when I was in the street, I would get nice shit for her. When she went to work, she'd have on Moschino this, Gucci that. She was upscale to the people at the job because she was getting money from me. But when there was no money between us, it just made every problem seem worse. Some of it was my fault, because the very first night my son came home, this chick I was messing with called the house. Tanisha picked up the phone and they got to arguing. I know that it was my fault the situation was taking place. I shouldn't have been messing around. But I was, and I got caught. The other bitch just told Tanisha everything that we had been doing over the summer while she was pregnant. The fight started for real that night and went on and on.

Still, we tried to work things out. Tanisha stopped going to school and moved to Far Rockaway, at the very end of the beach. Her mom had an apartment there and had just moved out, so we moved in. Our names weren't on the lease, but we were paying the rent. I wasn't comfortable with the idea, because things weren't right between us, but I wanted to give it a chance. I owed it to my son, because even if things didn't work out between his mother and me, I wanted to be able to look him in the face and tell him that I had put my best effort into giving him a family environment to grow up in.

Being out in Far Rockaway just added to the stress. I was in a new neighborhood and didn't have anyone around that I had grown up with. Anytime I wanted to hang out or do some business with Jay, I had to travel back to mainland Queens. Without a car, that was extremely difficult. The whole thing just put more pressure on the relationship.

When Tanisha started to work again, she told her mom about some guy at her job. What's crazy about it was that she had never gotten along with her mom at all. Her mom was looking out for us with the apartment because her daughter needed help, but the two of them were not friends. Still, Tanisha decided to tell her mother about this guy at work who likes her, owns a restaurant, and drives the same kind of Benz that I used to drive before I sold it to make music. So one day while Tanisha and I were arguing, her mother tells me, "My daughter ain't bad-looking. She can get somebody else."

"Well, tell her to get somebody else!" I said. "Leave me the fuck alone. You don't like the way I am? Leave me." I was getting into it with both of them all the time, and the living-together situation fell apart very quickly. I wound up moving back to my grandparents' house when my son was about six months old. Because Tanisha was working, I wound up taking care of my son most of the time. He was just a little baby—he couldn't even walk yet. My grandmother helped me out, but for the most part it was all on me. I sat home with him and worked on my music during the day and would take him to his mother's on the weekend. That's when I

would try to get into the studio and lay down the rhymes I had been working on all week.

Taking him out to Tanisha's house on the weekends was problem-
atic for me. I didn't have money for a cab, and it was hard to get him on a
dollar van with the stroller, the diaper bag, and his clothes. I had to wait for
the bus, and that hurt. It wasn't a big deal, because I was sacrificing for my
son, which is what a parent is supposed to do. But my pride was hurt. I was
in a bad space financially, and that threw me off. I was at the bus stop, seeing the kids who used to hustle for me now making money on their own,
and I knew they were laughing behind my back. I began to think I had
made the wrong decision. My rap dreams seemed farther away than ever.

One time, I got off the bus to give Tanisha our son and saw her
having a conversation with a kid she used to sleep with. I wasn't jealous,
but it pissed me off because I was not used to being in that situation, saddled with all sorts of baggage and watching my son's mother talking to her
ex-boyfriend. Even though we weren't officially together at that point, we
had not gone our separate ways, either. No matter how much we argued,
we still had to deal with our son, so it was hard to know exactly where our
relationship was at any given moment. Still, I didn't feel like it was at a
point where she would be talking to an ex when she knew I was coming
over. That was disrespectful. The kid she was talking to knew about me, so
when he saw me coming, he tried to leave, like, I'm staying out of it.

"You can stay," she told him. "It's not like that."

She just stayed there, talking to the kid. I dropped off our son and
the stroller and got back on the dollar van. I had nothing to say to her. But
the kid was so scared that he called me later and told me that he had
wanted to leave, but Tanisha told him to stay. "I ain't trying to get in between y'all," he said. "But she told me, 'It's not like that.'"

When I confronted Tanisha about it, she didn't even deny what
she had said, adding that she only told him that it was okay to hang
around because of the time we had argued when she saw me on the strip
with the other girl. She threw my own words back at me: "You said if you
saw me talking to somebody, you wouldn't act like that." In truth, I hadn't
acted the way she had, but I wasn't about to get into all of that with her. I
knew that her saying "It's not like that" to an ex-boyfriend was an open in-

vitation for more than just conversation. It's not that she did it, it's that she did it in my face. That told me our relationship was over.

A few weeks later, she asked me, "Why do I have to watch him on the weekend? That's my only time off." I couldn't believe what I was hearing. *So now it's a problem for me to even leave him with you at all.* She changed her position on that later, but I'll never forget her saying it. A mother who doesn't have time for her child? That's crazy. How am I supposed to ever trust her again? My mom was selling cocaine but she still made it her business to find time for me. Tanisha just wanted to hang out on the weekends. To this day, I look at her funny behind that. Even when we ended up back around each other again, it was real weird. I had feelings for her at first, but all the fighting took the love away.

"Fuck! Sometimes the rap game does remind me of the crack game . . ."

I met this executive from Columbia at the barbershop. He was getting a haircut and I told him that I had some songs to play for him. Everyone in the barbershop told him that I was hot. Even the people who may have laughed about me behind my back vouched for me because they figured that if I got signed, I would remember who had been there for me. The record exec brushed me off and said to wait until he was done with his haircut. I didn't like that, but what was I going to do? I still didn't have a record deal and I had put in far too much work to let my pride get in the way of possibly not being signed. When he went out to his car, I played him my song "The Hit." Markie Dee from the Fat Boys was with him and they were playing it in the ride, but they weren't really listening. While the music was playing, the guy from the record label was on his cell phone and Markie Dee was talking to somebody out the window. They didn't even pay attention.

When the song was finished, I asked them what they thought and they were like, "It's alright." I was pissed. I said, "Gimme my fuckin' tape. You niggas is mad old-school." They were offended that I would say that shit, but I didn't care. I knew that song was good. Too many people said it was one of the best tracks I had ever made, so I wasn't about to let their record-industry bullshit get to me—especially not after they had me waiting for so long.

A week later, the executive got my number through the kid who had cut his hair and called me at two o'clock in the morning. He said that he was going to the studio and would hook me up to work with the Track Masters, who at that time were the hottest producers in the game. I was cautious because it sounded too good to be true and I really didn't know this guy well enough for him to hook me up like that. I put it off to the next day, until I could check the guy's story and see it was safe.

When I got to the studio, I ran into Sha Money XL. Sha had been with JMJ, but he left and started working with the Track Masters. We had always been cool, so I wound up spending a lot of time hanging out with him and listening to beats. There were other artists signed to Track Masters up there, but they were complacent. They had been featured on other projects and wanted to act like the stars they were hanging around. They wanted to hang around in the studio and be *artists*. Not me; I was trying to work. I was hungry and trying to get my project off the ground. I didn't even have a record deal. They were signed to the Track Masters label. I was still signed to Jam Master Jay's production deal, but this was my chance to actually get on a label. I didn't have a plan B. I wasn't even thinking about signing to Track Masters. I just knew that if I got some Track Masters songs on my demo, then I'd get signed somewhere. I was up there for eighteen days and I left with thirty-six songs. I was doing two songs a day. I knew that wherever I went, somebody was going to pick me up and pay the Track Masters whatever it was going to cost to buy the songs.

The Track Masters liked the music enough to sign me, but I had to get off of Jam Master Jay's label first. I had explained myself to Jay ten times: I had been asking him for a release because I was bitter from not making any money on the music. He had refused to let me off, and when the Track Masters offer came, he asked me for fifty thousand dollars to get out of the contract. I was upset because he didn't spend that kind of money when we worked together. But I realized that if I hadn't taken the things he had shown me, it wouldn't have been possible for me to make a dollar. I would never have gotten the Track Masters deal before Jam Master Jay because I wasn't a good enough artist at that point. But the Track Masters deal was for only sixty-five thousand dollars. After lawyer's fees, I was left with five thousand dollars. I was like, Fuck— sometimes the rap game does remind me of the crack game! But at least in the crack game, you can lay on somebody when he plays you out of pocket. The music industry had a whole separate set of rules that I had to adjust to.

It was cool at first because I had already made thirty-six songs and I thought I was going to go back into the studio. But the Track Masters put me on hold for eight months. During that time, they transferred my contract to Columbia, the major label they were on, and I really got lost in the shuffle. That's when I got the idea to do "How to Rob." It wasn't a difficult song to write. I wrote it in about thirty minutes because it was what I was really feeling at the time. I was sitting back, broke, and watching all these MCs shine and show off their jewelry and cars. I was sitting back, thinking, I wish I could have that chain. And then I realized that I could have that chain if he comes to the 'hood and he ain't paying attention. The song just came out from there.

I knew that if I didn't make a record that made people ask, "Who is 50 Cent?" then I was wasting my time—the label wasn't going to do it for me. I had to make the kind of record that would make the entire music business say, "Who the fuck is this guy?" So I made the record, saying the name of everybody I wanted to rob. At that point, I was the only rapper who could have made "How to Rob," because I didn't have relationships with any of the MCs to the point where I'd have to get on the phone and explain myself. I wasn't calling anyone, because if I called one person, then I would have to call every single person on the record and clear it with them. I was like, It is what it is and if you got a problem with it, we can do whatever you want to do.

I got tired of the song real quick, but it really made its mark. Everybody who was somebody in the game had something to say about me. I saw that I was making my mark aggressively enough by the way people were acknowledging me immediately   not six months from the song, but right when the song came out. There were guys out with hit records no one was paying attention to. But all the top dogs had an issue with me, and I didn't even have an album out. The response to me helped put me in the game. The more they reacted, the bigger my name got. I couldn't pay for that kind of publicity—and my record label sure as hell wasn't going to.

I loved the guys who had something to say about me on a record. Big Pun, DMX, the Wu-Tang Clan. The best was Jay-Z when he responded at SummerJam. I saw him backstage and he said, "You know I'm about to go in on you, right?" I was like, What the fuck is he talking about? When he was performing, he stood in front of all of New York and dissed me: "I'm about a dollar, what the fuck is 50 Cent?" The next day I was on the radio station talking about the dis. A while later, I ran into Jay-Z at P. Diddy's restaurant, Justin's, and thanked him. He laughed at me. It probably tripped him out that I understood what was going on. I was thinking businesswise. I didn't give a fuck what he was saying. *Say whatever you want, motherfucker. Just say my name. That's all I need.*

*"Now you're getting personal.
It's not going to be easy
to cool this down . . ."*

A friend of mine robbed Ja Rule. That's how the beef originally started. My man robbed him for a chain, and then this guy named Brown came and got the chain back for Ja. Later, Ja saw me in a club with the kid who had robbed him. I went over to say "What's up" to Ja, and he acted like he had a problem with me. But I'm not the one who robbed him. *The nigga that robbed you is right there. You ain't got no problem with him, but you got a problem with me?* That pissed me off. At that point, I wasn't in a position to do or say anything; I was still a newborn. Even though I had put out "How to Rob," it was never released as a commercial single. It was only a promotional cut for DJs. So in reality, I had never sold a record, period. I didn't have anything to say, so I left it alone.

Later, he was filming a video on Jamaica Avenue and the whole 'hood was out there. I saw Ja again, so I acknowledged him, but he just moved right by me. I didn't give a fuck, but then he started running his mouth about me and telling people that I couldn't rap. Honestly, I didn't care if he said that I could rap or not. But seeing as I hadn't come out yet, he was sabotaging my fan base. If my own 'hood hadn't supported me to begin with, then it would have been that much harder to get off the ground. He was also leveraging relationships he had in the industry to keep people from working with me.

I was like, This nigga would never do that on the street. He was never on the street, he didn't hustle, he didn't bust his gun, he didn't do any of the stuff he talks about on his records. But because I was now a rapper, he felt that we were peers. So I went and made a song about him, "Your Life's on the Line." I didn't mention his name, but it was obvious who I was talking about. His crew was called Murder, Inc., and in the hook I sang "Scream 'Murder,' I don't believe you."

After I put out the song, Brown came by and told me to leave Ja alone. He said, "Leave that nigga alone. I'm eating, that nigga's my food." I was like, How do you refer to another man as your food? I didn't care; I made the song that I was supposed to make and left it at that.

Because "How to Rob" made a buzz, I was able to do a few shows. They weren't for much money, basically just enough to cover expenses, but they were shows and I was glad to have them. If nothing else, performing meant that my career was on the move. For one show in Atlanta, Ja Rule was on the bill with me. I didn't think anything of it, because I had already spoken to Brown about the situation. When I pulled up to my hotel before the show, I saw Ja standing outside, so I went over to talk to him and let him know everything was squashed. In my mind, we didn't have any problems. If I thought there was going to be a problem, I would have gone down there with, like, fifteen Brooklyn niggas and gone to the hardware store to make sure everybody had a knife by the time we made it there. But I was figuring, Fuck it, I already spoke to Brown, so it is what it is.

When I began talking to Ja, he started talking all crazy out his mouth. He was putting on a performance for his homeys, to build up his rep. But he was out of character, because he's not really a street nigga. He didn't know how to handle the conversation properly. He had this little baseball bat in his hand, which he was swinging around to make a point, but he really looked like a joker. Even if he had had the upper hand, there was no need for acting. He could have quietly said what he had to say and then gone back to his crew and told them, "Yeah, I showed him." He didn't get it. He felt that my coming to him to talk was out of fear, but it wasn't that. It was just respect for Brown and realizing that I had an opportunity to change my life. But Ja took my kindness for weakness and tried to play like the big man. He was talking crazy, but he wasn't even looking at me. He was looking toward his homeys and talking loud so they could hear him. But what he was really doing was begging me to punch him in the eye. His lips were flapping, but all I could hear coming out was, "Punch me in the eye. I deserve it. Please, punch me in the eye."

There are certain things I won't accept, no matter what. I was in the street too long to let that type of disrespect slide. So I did what he asked and clocked him right in the face. He had eight guys with him, and they ran over and piled on me. Eight guys. I was supposed to get peeled off that sidewalk and pushed into an ambulance. But that's not what happened. After it was all said and done, I walked away with his jewelry. I had popped his chain off while we were fighting and told him to come get it. But by that time, the police were coming and everybody dashed off. It was no big deal to me. I was willing to stay right there and mop his ass up, if he liked.

When I got back to New York, Brown approached me about what had happened. I explained the situation to him and he understood why it went down the way it did. He said he couldn't blame me and gave me a gold watch in order to get the chain back. But after that incident, I began to hustle again, because I wasn't sure if the rap thing was going to work out. At the time, Ja had more connections than I did in the industry, and I realized that I had burned a lot of bridges when I punched him in the face. There were no repercussions on the street level, but the industry was an entirely different beast.

I didn't want to go back to hustling, but at that point, I didn't feel as if I had a choice. I was leaving the game behind to rap, but rap was beginning to be too much of a hassle. Worse off, my name in the rap game was much larger than any funds it was generating. How would it look if I had the hottest street single in the city but I was still riding in dollar vans? Even though my music career was about to take off, I had to place myself in a position where people would want to deal with me. No one wants to do business with someone who looks like he needs help. Successful people only want to do business with people who look like they have something to offer. The two go hand in hand. If I was going to make it in the rap game, then I had to go back to the crack game.

//////////////////

When I got back into selling drugs, I was even more aggressive at it than I had been. I had to be. I had lost so much time that people were questioning me, so I had to make a few examples. This rubbed a lot of people the wrong way. A lot of people had gotten comfortable while I was gone, but I wasn't paying them any mind. I was picking up right where I had left off. I wanted to take the strip back; it made no sense to go for anything less.

I gathered a crew and brought in reinforcements from Brooklyn. It was just like old times. The game fit me like I had never left. Almost. During my time away, a few older guys who ran things back in the day had come back from jail. They were looking at me like I was too young to be trying to take over, but I didn't give a fuck about any of them. Their time had passed. Everybody eventually grows up and comes into their own. I was like, Fuck that, I'm a grown man. But the older guys looked at me like, I coulda had this nigga—I coulda had a kid his age. And he's tellin' me, "Fuck you." That was the beginning of a lot of problems.

One night, Kyle and Sonny got into a fight over a girl. Kyle and Sonny were older guys with heavy reps and a lot to lose if their crews got into a war. But there was honor at stake, because the woman in question was Sonny's girlfriend when he went to jail. Yet when Sonny came out, she was with Kyle. Sonny felt that Kyle shouldn't have been with his girl, out of respect, but Kyle didn't agree, so they decided to settle things hand to hand, like the old school. They squared up, and Kyle lumped Sonny up something awful.

At this point, I was burning the candle at both ends—I was in the studio as much as I was in the street. I missed the fight, but when I came around, everyone told me what had happened. Later that night, I saw Sonny on the other strip and went to talk to him. During the whole conversation, I was staring in his face. "What the fuck you looking at?" he asked.

"I'm looking to see if you got lumped up," I said. "Niggas said you got lumped up by Kyle, so I was just looking to see if that was true." Sonny couldn't believe it. He made like he wanted to get at me, but he knew my reputation as a boxer, so he kept his distance. There was a crowd of people around, and it would have been embarrassing for him to get beaten up twice in the same night—especially if the second thumping came from a kid fifteen years younger than him.

"You better watch your mouth," he told me.

"Or what?" I taunted him. "You ain't gonna do shit but sit there and get your ass beat again, chump. You supposed to be some big shot, and you got your ass whupped. If that nigga Kyle put his hands on me, I woulda beat his ass under the pavement."

Everyone was silent, and Sonny just walked away. Later that night, Godfather called me and told me that I was getting out of hand. "You're disrespecting the wrong people," he said.

"Who?" I asked. "Sonny? Fuck him."

"You publicly dissed Sonny and you dissed Kyle," he said. "That's too much, man. You're doing strong business and I can respect that, but now you're getting personal. It's not going to be easy to cool this down."

Godfather arranged a sit-down with everyone involved, but he had scheduled it on a day that I had a studio session, so I skipped on the meeting. I really didn't give a fuck about those old guys anyway. I felt the tension in the air, but it didn't matter to me. My label wasn't giving me a lot of studio time, and that was more important to me than some old gangster's ego. I figured if I made the right music, I would blow and wouldn't even have to worry about those motherfuckers. The funny thing is, trouble found me that night in the studio.

///////,,,,,,,,//////

I was recording at the Hit Factory in Manhattan, and Ja Rule was recording in a separate studio. I guess he was still upset about my laying a pounding on him in Atlanta, because he and his crew rushed into my studio while I was recording. Someone snuck in and turned out the lights and a fight broke out. The fight was so quick I didn't even know what happened. They ran in, threw some sucker punches, and ran out. I wasn't sure what was going on, so I got out and hopped in a cab and went home. When I was in the backseat of the taxi, I realized that I was bleeding from my gut. I figured that I must have bumped into a piece of recording equipment or something. When I got home, my grandmother told me that she had heard that I was stabbed in a studio. I lifted up my shirt to show her the nick, and she cleaned it off with peroxide. "I told you that you can't keep doing bad things and not expect them to come back to you," she said.

I told her that I was just minding my own business in the studio when some guys ambushed me, but she didn't believe me. A few hours later, my phone started ringing and people were telling me they heard that Ja Rule's crew had stabbed me in the studio. That's how I found out who it was. But it was wack to me. It felt like a publicity stunt, because everyone knew what happened before I did. And the cut wasn't even anything to brag about. They ran in, turned out the lights, and I left with a prick. That was real corny. A guy can get into a fight at a club and wind up needing 150 stitches to keep his face together, so their turning out the lights and doing all that dumb shit didn't serve a purpose. If they were that gangster, they would have allowed me to see who it was. The only reason I even went to the hospital was because, the next morning, my grandmother wanted me to make sure the cut wasn't infected. It had stopped bleeding, but she wanted me to double-check, so I did. When I got to the hospital, they put in three stitches, prescribed some antibiotics, and sent me home.

Then Godfather called and told me that he was upset about my missing the meeting. He said he went to a lot of trouble to set everything up and I hadn't even given him the courtesy of a phone call. He told me I was on my own. I felt like everything was closing in on me. I was going against the odds, but I thought I could beat them.

*"The shooter was on me,
emptying bullets . . ."*

The driver was waiting for me out front in the car with his girlfriend. He didn't see anything out of the ordinary. I walked out of the house, looked both ways, and hopped in. The driver saw my chain and wondered where the diamond-cross pendant was.

"I ain't rockin' it," I said. "Why? You think I should rock it?"

"Yeah."

"You don't think this one's hot?"

"That one's on fire. That's why I think you should rock the cross and let me rock that one."

"You a funny nigga," I laughed.

We sat in the car for a minute. I waited for him to pull off. After a minute, he looked over his shoulder. "Oh, shit. You still here? I thought you went back to get the other chain."

I went back in the house, put on the diamond cross, and decided to get some hardware in case we ran into any problems due to the jewelry. I grabbed a jacket to carry the pistols I pulled from the backyard and made a light jog to the car, with the guns in the jacket, the jacket in my arm, the chain in my hand. This time I didn't look both ways.

Another car eased up the block and stopped, but it didn't register at the time. I slid into the backseat. I felt someone coming over my shoulder but saw no one there. The other car resumed rolling. When I handed the chain to the driver, the shooter was sneaking up on my left side. I want to believe that I saw it coming at that point. But if I had seen it coming, then I wouldn't have gotten shot, would I?

The shooter was on me, emptying bullets. I jumped. I felt my legs on fire and fell back down. The shooter stuck his hand deeper in the window, still bucking. I reached for the jacket in my lap. I pointed the pistol at the shooter, but the gun wasn't cocked. There was nothing in the chamber. A bullet tore into my face and my mouth exploded. Another slug blew up my hand before the driver finally pulled off.

CHAPTER 21

"I had to go to the gym just to

get my legs back in it . . ."

After I got shot nine times at close range and didn't die, I started to think that I must have a purpose in life, like, I have to be here for a reason. I was wondering, How was this nigga standing over me this close, bangin' off nine times and can't finish? All that fancy footwork; he's like Allen Iverson going to the basket, shakin' niggas—but he can't get the basket in. There was a bullet wound in my face, but it didn't stop me or change me or nothing. It was just a tooth missing. How much more damage could that shell have done? Give me an inch in this direction or that one, and I'm gone.

The situation with those shots going off didn't have anything to do with hip-hop. It stemmed from me not cooperating with the niggas in the streets. I was on my own page and felt like niggas should do what I wanted them to do. They felt like I should be doing what they wanted me to do. And that's when the shots went off.

After I got shot, everybody I had differences with was still out on the street. They were available, but I couldn't get my hands on them. They weren't accessible to me, but they were out there. Everybody was there except the actual shooter; he got killed two weeks after I had gotten shot. He was from Brooklyn, and the guys I knew from Brooklyn knew who it was. He wasn't even down with the crew that shot me—he was a freelancer. Had I paid him first, he would've shot those other niggas for me. I knew everything about the situation right after it happened. I was able to find out because, like I said, reputation is the cornerstone of power. These guys were supposed to be gangstas, so they needed people to know *why* they're the kind of nigga you didn't want to fuck with. They needed people to know, "Yeah, I did that." Even if it's within a community that won't say anything, they needed it known, otherwise it's worthless.

CHAPTER 22

I knew exactly what was popping. I got all kinds of phone calls. Some people were just trying to have a conversation with me, to see where my head was at. They knew that ever since I was small, I would let my gun pop if there was a problem, no questions asked. Some people were just trying to get information. Some people were offering resources to respond to the situation. They gave me the go-ahead to strike back, saying, "If you make a move on these guys right now, no one's going to do a thing." But I didn't know who to trust. Basically, I was on my own. I just fell back because I didn't know what position my crew was in. I didn't know who was going to react the right way.

I think regular people who haven't been in that environment might go to counseling and therapy. But that wasn't really necessary for me. I did things to people and got away with it, so I looked at it like what goes around comes around. I wasn't all of a sudden scared to leave my house or anything like that.

I wouldn't let people come to see me in the hospital because I was bent up a little bit. I was the strongest nigga from my section, so my crew looked to me for answers to things. I couldn't let them see me in a compromising space. When something had to be dealt with, I was the one who gave them the heart to deal with it. If they saw me in the hospital, then they could have fallen apart. I could tell them, "Nah, son, I'm all right," but I couldn't move my legs, because my legs were shot the fuck up; I couldn't move my hand, because I had pins sticking out where a bullet went through my thumb and came out at the top of my pinkie; I had a hole in my face and braces in my mouth, so I couldn't even speak clearly. No matter how many times I would have mumbled, "Nah, son, I'm all right," they would have looked at me like, "Damn, this nigga's fucked up." That may have altered them to the point where they felt like they had to go do something else. They may have turned into different people after seeing me in a situation where I didn't look so strong. So the only people who were able to come see me were my grandparents, my son, and his mom.

My hip was killing me. It was fractured. The hip is a major bone— I couldn't even sit down right. That shit was crazy. I didn't have any pain-killer medication—no drugs, no nothing. I should have had some, but they didn't give me a prescription when I left the hospital, and I never went back. That was the first time I'd been in a hospital since I was born, besides the time I went and got the three stitches. I had never been in the hospital any other time. I don't like hospitals. I stayed there for thirteen days, and that was enough for me.

When I got out of the hospital, I was out of town for a little bit. I was supposed to go to physical therapy, but I didn't like it. That shit hurt too much. With my hand, they were bending my thumb all the way back to keep scar tissue from developing around the bones. They were pushing the shit all the way down, and it would hurt like a motherfucker. I'd come from there and be sore. So after I did it once or twice, I didn't ever go back. I started doing my own rehab; I'd sit there and fuck with my hand myself and I enrolled in a gym. I had lost so much weight. First off, I lost weight being in the hospital those thirteen days. Then I lost more, because I was fed through an IV for six more weeks. My jaw was still wired shut, so I was sipping hot macaroni and cheese or tuna fish and milk that had been run through a blender. I had gone from 230 pounds to 167. I was real skinny. I had to go to the gym just to get my legs back in it. The majority of the shots were in my legs—a lot of flesh wounds. I started out just walking. I was doing a lot of walking because I was at a place where you couldn't just walk around the block or hop in a cab. And then I went to the gym to get on the treadmill to walk.

I was in the Poconos. My son's maternal grandmother lived out in the Poconos, so we stayed at her place with my son's mom while I got myself together. But as I said, Tanisha and her mom had problems. They'd be going at each other for no reason. They argued like people who hate each other, not like a mother and daughter. It got to the point that we couldn't stay there. I'm looking at my son's mom like, How stupid can you be? How you gonna fight when you don't have an alternative? Her brain should have told her that it was not that serious, like, I gotta at least find me a new place to stay before we fight. But she just didn't have that self-preservation instinct. She just let it rip, like *rrrraaaaaaaaw* with her fucking mouth. Her mom was like, "Y'all gotta go." She had to go back to New York to stay with her grandmother for a while.

I stayed with Tanisha's mom while I was looking for a place for us to stay. But Tanisha came back and told her mom, "Oh, you think he likes you? He don't fuckin' like you. He's just doing what he gotta do to get his situation straight." This is my son's mother telling her mother that. I couldn't fucking believe it. I'm like, "You stupid bitch. Now we still gotta get a place to live. We can't live at your grandmom's house in New York. Where would we be, in the living room?!?" Her grandmother had a one-bedroom apartment over on Highland Avenue in Jamaica. It wasn't big enough for her and it wasn't safe for me. It made no sense, but Tanisha just didn't grasp that shit.

Luckily, I was able to get a condo out there. I had signed a publishing deal on the hospital bed. The deal was for $250,000; I got $125,000 in advance and the other buck twenty-five was supposed to come when the album came out. After all of the lawyers fees and stuff like that, I walked away from that with $85,000. I got the crib and started working out because I was still fucked up physically. I was able to walk, but I was still having a hard time. But I rode a motorcycle to the gym and spent a lot of time riding on the little pedal bikes.

I went back to working on my music. So, I'm going to the gym and coming back, trying to get myself together, and working on my music. This went on for about a year and some change, then the money started to get low. It was simple math: The money was going out only, not coming in. It actually would have been cheaper to have bought the place instead of renting it.

I told my son's mom, "You gotta go to work," because she'd go to school, but then she'd come back and sit around all day. I told her to get a job, but she looked at me like, You always tellin' me to look for work, but you ain't doin' no work. She didn't respect what I was doing. The music shit didn't seem like work to her; she'd just see me in front of the radio all day doing nothing. At this point I had stopped writing my lyrics down and had a large portion of them in my head. So in her eyes, I was just fucking around in front of the music all day. To her, I wasn't doing anything; I was just listening to the radio. To me, I was putting together what is now called *Get Rich or Die Trying*. I was like, "This is my fucking shit right now." But she was like, "You don't look like you doing nothin' to me."

I think it was around that time that I basically knew we were a wrap. To an outsider looking in, it could look like I left when I started blowing up. But in her head and in her heart, she's got to know that we'd been having problems forever.

"The only business model I had was from selling drugs, so that's how I marketed my product . . ."

Getting shot wasn't the worst thing that had happened to me. The worst thing that happened to me was not knowing what I was going to do after I had gotten shot. I wasn't sure what I was going to do with my life. I had decided that I was going to do music instead of the shit I was doing in the street, but after I got shot up, the people I had been doing business with weren't taking my calls. I was calling them and saying, "I'm ready. I got my shit back together," but no one cared. Everything just shifted. Everyone turned his back. The difference between business and people who pretend to be friends was showing.

Sitting back and watching people sell records hurt more than being shot. The shots passed—I was out of the hospital in thirteen days and healed up months later. But over a year later, the record company was still not in a position to do anything with me. They dropped the ball the first time, and after the shooting, they had even less of an idea of what to do with me. They didn't even know that it was possible for someone to get shot the way I did. To the people who were in control of my career, what happened to me only happens on TV; it's a news story. It's not something they have to deal with in a real way.

I took to building myself up. It wasn't a long process, because I was ready, willing, and able to work. It took a while to get out of my contract, but once I did, everything was on me. Every time it's on me, I pull through. Whenever it gets left up to another dude to bring to the table what he's supposed to bring to the table, I always fall short.

I was back in touch with Sha Money XL. He showed up at the hospital the day I got shot and called my grandmother and kept in touch all the time I was away. He had a spot out in Long Island, with a studio in the basement. I didn't have finances at that point, so I basically traveled in and out of New York, going from the gym to the gun range to the studio to the gym to the gun range to the studio to the gym to the gun range. By this time, I had become so acclimated to going to the gym that it became a habit to be in there, not even to necessarily lift weights, but to box, hop on the treadmill, or whatever. My body was back up to speed, though I would have a slight limp for a long time. I would go to a firing range located a few hours from the city, to keep my aim up to par. I was never going to be caught unawares again.

I started to work on music, putting it out on mix-tapes. The only business model I had was from selling drugs, so that's how I marketed my product. I knew that the only way to get into any market is to give out free samples. I had to build up a clientele before I could see a profit. I had to invest in my brand.

The first song I put out was "Fuck You," telling the niggas who shot me, "Fuck you." My situation was a public situation—people knew that I had gotten banged up. When they heard me say that, I think it made them look at me in a different light. Out the gate I was like "fuck you" to the niggas who shot me. That was new. Most of the niggas out there who talk gangsta and thug shit in raps don't really want to be a part of the stuff they're putting on their records. They're not ready for guns to bang off on some real shit. If niggas were to come see about them and shoot them nine times, I bet money those rappers would lose interest in the music real fast. But I didn't let that shit stop me. Outside of music was the 'hood. I was leaving the 'hood, and look at what happened. What was I supposed to do, go back to the 'hood? It already came back to me. It was the same thing at that point. I was like, Fuck it. If it's gonna come, it's gonna come.

The mix-tape DJs loved "Fuck You." They were hooked, so I started supplying them with freestyles. At first, I played by the rules and did exclusives for the DJs. I'd go into the studio with a DJ and do something specifically for that DJ. But then I just started to give everyone the same freestyle—I syndicated myself. I wanted to saturate the market, and there was no way I could do that by catering to each specific DJ. I decided to make the songs myself and just ship them out.

I had the contact info for about fifty or sixty DJs across the country. I reached out to them and let them know what I was doing, so they wouldn't feel like I was just sending them music. I made them feel like they were a part of something. I let them know that I'd give them every freestyle I made, and I'd give some of them exclusives and switch up who got what first, so it wasn't like I was playing favorites. I took the "Weird Al" Yankovic approach and started remaking songs. I didn't give a fuck whose beat it was—if it was halfway decent, I would jump on it and remake your song. I took shit from Wu-Tang, Talib Kweli, Angie Martinez, Raphael Saadiq, Next, whoever. I didn't have to like you to like your beat.

My approach to the mix-tape circuit altered the whole hip-hop industry. Now everyone's following in my footsteps; everybody's putting out their own mix-tape CDs and using my format, as far as doing freestyles in a song format. What's funny is that I did it because I had no other option. If I had had the money, I would have just pressed vinyl and gone to college and mix-show radio. But the money wasn't available and I had to do what was accessible. I had the notoriety of being on a major label, and my being shot was a selling point. In the street, niggas knew. Even people who didn't know my music knew my story: 50 Cent? Oh, yeah, that's the guy who got shot. When they heard me come back on the mix-tape circuit, they thought, He must have an album coming. The bootleggers were even using me as their selling point. When I heard one of them say, "Yo, I got the new 50 Cent on here," I knew I was on to something. A bootlegger said that to me in Manhattan. An African dude on Canal Street looked me in the face and said, "I got the new 50 Cent." If he hadn't said that to me, I'm not sure I would've gone in the direction of putting out my own mix-tapes. But when he told me that, I knew it meant that the people who came to him were asking for the new 50 Cent. The bootleggers don't listen to the music, they only know what people are requesting. There were a lot of established artists on that tape, but 50 Cent was the selling point. At that time, I had done about six DJ Clue tapes, Kay Slay tapes, DJ Absolut, Kool Kid—everybody who was putting something out and I could get my hands on. But after talking to the bootlegger, I decided I was going to put myself out on a collector's edition of my own.

At that point, I wasn't traveling much. I wasn't doing shows, radio, none of that stuff. I was prepared to sacrifice all that and just put out my records. That way, whoever saw me would feel as if he were seeing a star for real. Besides, there was still too much going on, and I didn't have the resources to secure myself in the way I needed to be secured in the public view. I wasn't getting involved in any more rap beef at that point. The real shit I had to deal with was enough for me. The rap beef was corny. A lot of rappers were trying to portray themselves as John Gotti or Al Capone or some big gangster. It was all, If you dis me, I'm gonna do this to you. I was like, Okay, let's do it then. That was my situation. I had nothing to lose. So if a rapper was putting himself out there like he was Supergangster, it would have been better for him to keep 50 Cent's name out of his mouth, because I would have shown him real quick that he was full of shit. Or if he wasn't full of shit, he was going to have to blow off my head to stop me. It made more sense for me to avoid confrontation by minding my own business, because we both would have been out the game. I'm not saying that I'm the most gangsterest nigga or that I was surrounded by the most gangster-est niggas, but I didn't have anything to lose. There was nothing that could come my way at that point that I hadn't already dealt with.

Truth is, there's no such thing as a "gangsta rapper," because no one can be a *gangsta* and a *rapper* at the same time. A rapper can have gangsta ties, he can know gangstas, but he can't be a gangsta. He has to be an artist if he's going to be an artist. I was still trying to figure out which I was going to be. It's like I had a microphone in one hand and my Ruger in the other. I wanted to be an artist, but there were complications. I couldn't do shows because I would have had to broadcast where I was going to be. I couldn't go on the radio because niggas knew where the radio station was and probably would have been waiting outside to tear off my head when I was done. It was better for everyone to hit the brakes: just slow down and eat. Because if anybody felt like he wanted to take it there, I would have. If a nigga told me that he was going to do something to me and I believed him, then he would have had a problem. I don't openly disrespect people I believe. If someone said something about me and I thought he was a stand-up guy with a reputation that he could live up to, then I had nothing to say back. He would get dealt with because he should have known that he shouldn't have said what he said.

I didn't have a plan B in the music industry. If the music didn't go right, then I was going to go back to the 'hood. It wasn't possible for me to take every single block, so I was just going to take every single dollar out of niggas' pockets every time I saw them.

That was my mind-set at the time. I was making two records a day—all day, every day. But all those records were records that would make people want to go out and kill, just because they were reflective of my state of mind after being shot. But I knew I had to make different music; I had to have the whole range of emotion in my music to be taken seriously. I had to be happy, upset, funny, everything. Everyone knew I could be angry, but I had to let people hear me sound as if I didn't have a care in the world. I couldn't pretend like I was Angry Man all the time. That's not reality. In the course of one day, the average person is going to go through different emotions. As an artist, I had to change emotionally in my work so that people could really enjoy my music as they changed. When someone's feeling happy, I should have a happy song for him; when he's pissed off, I should have a song for that, too. I didn't want to meet with any record labels until I had the records that they were looking for. And I knew what they were looking for: radio records.

Making radio records was harder than the other stuff. It's not just about having an R&B hook with three verses. That's good for a hit but not necessarily smart for your career. For a radio record to work for me, it has to be a reflection of who I am and how I feel about things. If I had had a big record that didn't tie into what I am, it wouldn't have helped me. "Wanksta," the record that became my first radio hit, wasn't meant to be a radio hit. I didn't go into the studio and say, "Here's the radio hit." I was just doing songs every day and that one took. I think that sometimes the best ideas just fall into your lap.

When I came up with the name G-Unit, I was watching TV, watching music videos. I saw Gorillaz, that cartoon group that was out at the time with the song that went: "I got sunshine in a bag / I'm useless, but not for long / The future is coming on." That made sense to me. I had already been vibing on the military because of the discipline, loyalty, and code of honor. From there, I went with "G-Unit." I had known Tony Yayo and Lloyd Banks my whole life. We all grew up together, but we hadn't rapped together or anything like that. Yayo was still out there hustling— hard. Banks was a baby; he was only eighteen, but he had already made his name on local mix-tapes. I pulled him right off the stoop, took him to my grandmother's house, and let him know I was sticking with the rap thing and putting a crew together.

When I got them in the studio, they were *green*. Yayo was rhyming with his back to the mike and Banks was screaming all over the place. They were so used to rhyming in the street that they had to be retrained for records. Sha Money wasn't my manager at that time, but he was handling a lot of managerial duties. He got me a five-page spread in a national magazine before I really had any music out in the streets. That bugged me out, because when I was on a major label, I was only getting one-page stories. But now I had a full feature with no album to speak of. Do you now how crazy that is?

I met Young Buck while we were putting the mix-tapes together. At the time, Buck was rolling with Juvenile. Juvenile was working from a tour bus and came to New York. When we hooked up, I had Banks and Yayo with me, and Juvenile had his crew, UTP. Rappers really don't freestyle with each other. Once they've sold some records, it's about money. But when I hooked up with Juvenile, we all started freestyling. We wound up recording a couple of songs together, because Juvenile had a studio on his bus at the time. Buck played me some records, and I felt where he was coming from, so we parted that situation with the understanding that whoever got signed first was going to reach out to the other.

I got DJ Whoo Kid to put together my first CD because he had been the first DJ to put my music on a mix-tape when no one else would. I got the photographer from the magazine to do a full photo shoot. Back then, no one put any thought into the artwork on mix-tapes, but I treated my mix-tapes with the same attention that I would have a real album. I knew the importance of packaging. I didn't take a Kodak moment from out of the machine and use that as the artwork. I did a long photo shoot with about five different color schemes, figuring that would last about five mix-tapes if I used a different color scheme every time. And because the quality was so clear, even when it got bootlegged, it still looked better than most of the stuff on the shelves. If there are ten mix-tapes in the store, five of them look like they cost two dollars to make. Then, there are maybe three that look decent. But two will stand out. And those two are going to sell the most.

I put eight new songs at the beginning of the CD and used a lot of the material that had already generated a reaction near the end. It sold out in like two days. The reaction was so good that I didn't know when I should release another one. Three weeks later, I dropped another one and that one sold out, too. The way the streets responded to my music was crazy. You heard G-Unit material coming out of every car, every open apartment window, every barbershop—any and everywhere niggas listened to music. In the streets, people I had never seen before in my life were shouting, "G-G-G-G-G-Unit!" The next thing I knew, they were playing the songs on the radio. First, they would just be played during the mixshows; then, in regular rotation; then the songs were making it into the nightly countdowns. That was unheard-of. Mix-tape songs on the radio? That wasn't supposed to happen.

I may have been doing good in the streets as far as recognition, but there's no money in mix-tapes and I still wasn't able to do any shows. All the notoriety didn't take my problems in the 'hood away. If anything, it made them worse, because some guys paid good money to have me killed, and not only did I have the nerve to live, but they had to hear my voice every time they stepped out of their house. I know they didn't like that. But I just kept on making music. It was all I could do at that point.

When the calls did start coming in from record labels that wanted to meet me, I traveled the only way I traveled at the time: with a bulletproof vest. The record executives looked at me like I was crazy. I made them uncomfortable, but I could live with that. Being dead, I couldn't live with. All of them were scared. One guy looked like he had shit his pants; a chick from Universal could hardly talk straight. But one executive was cool, real O.G. He didn't seem phased at all, like, Nice vest. Does it have a deflective shield? Because of the interest I was generating on the streets, they all put deals on the table. One label actually came back with a very nice monetary offer, but it had a terrible history of selling hip-hop. If I had signed with that label, I would have basically cashed in my chips and gone back to the 'hood with the guns and the crack. And that's what I was trying to avoid.

"I can't take my vest?
Well, I can't make the meeting . . ."

I got a call from my lawyer regarding Eminem and Dr. Dre on a Friday evening. Saturday morning, I was flying out to L.A. What's wild is that I nearly missed the meeting because I went through the airport security check with my vest on. When the alarm went off, I felt like I was back in high school with the wrong tennis shoes. I half expected to see green tops drop out of my carry-on bag. I had gotten on planes with my vest before, so I knew that as long as I removed the deflective shield I could walk through without a problem. I had taken the metal plate out of the front and I walked through, but I had forgotten to take off my belt buckle. The security lady waved me over. She touched the vest through my clothes and asked what it was. I told her it was a back brace. She looked at me like I was bin Laden's nephew.

I was standing on the side when a supervisor came over. I showed him the back of the vest and told him that it was a back brace. He says, "All right. Well, take your back brace off and put it in your bag, Mr. 50 Cent." It was a blessing that the person acknowledged who I was and gave me a break, because I could have been sitting in the police precinct over some bullshit and I wouldn't have the meeting with Dre and Em. They were already thinking, Damn, we don't wanna buy a problem but let's meet him, let's see where his head is at. A no-show would have made them think, Wow, he missed the meeting—he wasn't able to come because he got caught in the airport with a bulletproof vest. That would have made a *great* first impression. I put the vest in my carry-on bag and went through. That shit just happened out of habit because I was like, I'm not goin' nowhere without my vest on. If it came down to leaving the vest or missing the meeting, I'd probably be in the streets right now. *What? I can't take my vest? Well, I can't make the meeting. You comin' to New York anytime soon?*

When I got off the plane, I went straight to the set where Eminem was filming *8 Mile*. It was a weird experience: With all the other meetings, I was looking for someone who could see what I was trying to do and put some money and support behind it. But Dr. Dre and Eminem were different. I wanted to impress them. But before I had a chance to say anything, Em tried to sell himself to me. I was like, "I know who you are. You're the guy with the number one album in the country. You break some sort of record every time you put out an album. What the fuck are you trying to impress *me* for?" Dr. Dre came up in a blue Lamborghini, blasting one of my tapes. (It may have been a gray Lamborghini—I've never seen Dre drive the same car twice.) When he got out of the car, all he said was, "You ready to make history together?" Dre was pointing out songs from the mix-tape that he liked. He was like, "I want this on the album. I want that on the album." I was like, "You gotta be kidding me. Those are freestyles!"

I knew before I met with them that I was going to sign with those guys. I knew as soon as I got that phone call. The concerns I had about signing with the other labels weren't a factor in dealing with them. They knew how to sell records, they had money, and I wasn't worried about Mr. "Fuck tha Police" and Mr. "I Just Don't Give a Fuck" censoring my material. But it still took me a while to get to the point where I could totally trust their judgment. Now I'll just change something that Dre asks me to change, because I know that he's thinking of something he's going to do to the song that I don't know about. With "In da Club," when I said, "My flow, my show brought me the dough, that brought me all my fancy things," I just said it. Dre said, "Do it a bit *lighter.*" So I made it more singsongy, like a bridge. I didn't know how it was going to turn out, but he knew that he was hearing something that wasn't in the track yet. It only took us about an hour to record, but Dre will sit with a song for a few days to perfect it. I learned that you might not get the best material possible out of him if you don't trust him enough to change something.

When it comes to Eminem and Dr. Dre, I won't do anything that they're uncomfortable with when we do business. I remember exactly where I just came from and understand who helped me get where I'm at now. I'll do almost anything for Dre and Em. When they signed me, they could have been purchasing a big problem. I could've went in another direction, fucked everything up, and made them look crazy. Instead I kept working and turned my career into what it is now. Em, he's about winning. He's the one that went to Dre and said, "Are you interested in doing this with me?" And Dre said, "Yeah." Em went with me and he made it all happen. Bottom line. A lot of my success is credited to Eminem, regardless of how people look at it or feel about it. He did make the situation happen.

Em and I speak more than Dre and I do. I think Dre might be cynical as far as trust issues go. I know I am, so it takes a while for me to forge a bond with someone. Plus, he's a grown man, married with kids. He doesn't get excited about the same shit that I get excited about. He makes music *about* it, but he isn't going to *do* it at this point in his life. Em gets excited about everything. It's like he's going through his beginning all over again with me. He's like, "I know you're never gonna forget the first time you go to Japan! Yo, you wanna go to Japan? Let's got to Japan! Let's go to the U.K.!" So we go to Japan, we go to the U.K., Amsterdam, Germany, Paris, Switzerland, all the different places. I was looking at it: *Yo, we at a soccer field—70,000 motherfuckers out there, and we're performin'.* Japan was the first time I ever got to see music break the language barrier. There were people singing my songs in the club, word for word. But when the music stopped, I couldn't talk to them because they spoke another language. That's crazy.

I didn't even have an album out and I was touring the world. People didn't know English, but they knew the words to my mix-tape songs. That's when I really knew I was on the right track. To be accepted by my 'hood was one thing, but when I started crossing cultural barriers by just being myself, all the trials and tribulations seemed worth it.

*"I'm telling you it's gonna be crazy
when you come out.
They gonna be all over you
when you come this time . . ."*

I was on my way to the studio in Long Island when I heard that Jam Master Jay had been murdered. A mutual friend called and was like, "Jay just got killed." I was like, "What? Are you sure?" He said, "Yeah, I'm sure. I'm right here." I was thinking, This guy said Jay got killed. What the fuck? It wasn't tallying up in my head how the fuck that was possible. I mean, *for what?* He's not out there. If you heard that that happened to 50 Cent, it would be a little more believable, considering my past. It is what it is. It's karma. But Jay's situation was shocking because of how it went down. It felt weird because I had spoken with Jay two days before he got killed. He was talking about some film opportunities that he had. He was excited. He was telling me, "Yo, I'm telling you, it's gonna be crazy when you come out. They gonna be all over you when you come this time." Everything that he said would happen to me surrounding my album happened to me, but surrounding his death instead of my album. That's when the whole shit with the media really started.

What was wild was that I was supposed to meet him—not me myself physically, but Sha Money—to pick up a script about an hour before he got hit. Sha never made the meeting to pick up the script because there had been a discrepancy. He was calling to tell me what was going on; in the middle of that, I got a call on the other line: "Jay got hit." I'm like, "Aw, nah. Get the fuck out of here."

That night, I went into the studio and dedicated a song to Jay. I was supposed to perform in the city afterward. I was going to dedicate the show to his memory, but the police shut the club down. The police tried to make it look like I didn't do the performance because I didn't want to go out, but they're the ones who shut it down. They said that they would arrest me if I came to the sidewalk. They thought that whoever shot Jam Master Jay was after me. They had a theory that somebody killed Jay to send 50 a message. In their heads, it was like: If 50 comes to the show, something's definitely gonna happen. These guys, they don't care, because 50's gonna come anyway, but he's gonna bring a bunch of people with guns down here and we're going to have a terrible situation in this club. So let's squash the whole situation right now by saying there won't be a show.

They tied me up in that situation because the place where Jay got killed is three minutes away from where I was shot. Before Jay, I was the last person in the music business to get shot. The police knew about my arrests, and they knew about the shootings that took place—niggas were saying that it was my little soldiers. My popularity had grown past the street shit. Niggas in the neighborhood were running around saying "G-Unit" even though they didn't have any affiliation to the music or to me. They're just from that neighborhood and they wanted to say that because that's their 'hood. So when something happens, someone says that G-Unit shot up the party. And the police will hear it. If it's being said in the street, believe that it's being said in the precinct. And when you say "50 Cent" in that precinct, those cops go, "He's not an angel. He's not the worst we've seen, but he's no angel. We know who you're talking about, and it can't be in a good light."

When you have a dead body and you don't have any answers, you start looking around. The answer to why that body is there is usually between friends and enemies. First they run through a list of enemies. A guy like Jam Master Jay didn't have a bad aura around him, so he didn't have a whole bunch of enemies. But when they start going through his friends, they come up with 50 Cent and go, "Oh, do you think that somebody would do something to Jam Master Jay to send 50 Cent a message?" This is an idea they came up with early in the game; it was an early assumption. So when they had no answer and the press was in their face, they had to make up some shit: "We believe this has something to do with 50 Cent." They weren't reporting that they had any leads, because their only lead was that they had no leads. But instead of saying that, they said, "We're investigating links to 50 Cent." They had me on the eleven o'clock news, and I was like, Huh? I just heard about this at seven o'clock. Then the newspaper hit: "50 Cent, 50 Cent, 50 Cent" all over the place, tying me to that shit. I still have no idea what the fuck they were talking about.

They canceled my show that night because they felt like there was going to be a problem. They said that the kind of people who would kill Jay to send me a message might have been out to kill me that night. A police officer told me, "We know from valid sources that there's a hit on you." But he didn't tell me that they had made an arrest. I knew they were only there to talk to me for information. If you're telling me that "valid sources" say there's a hit on me, then your next statement should be, "And we picked up the guy." But if you tell me that and then you look at me to see what I'm gonna say, I'll be like, Excuse me, I gotta go. I know what the fuck you're here for. *You're telling me people dislike me or might not want to see me do good or there might be a hit on me? Tell me something I don't know.* It didn't matter to me either way. It wasn't anything that I hadn't been dealing with

Cops make me uncomfortable. It's not a positive thing to see them. Usually, when they're around, they're around to take me or somebody around me to jail. The police department isn't there to de-escalate a situation. They're there to clean up the mess. After somebody's killed, they want to find out who shot the dead guy. They don't want to get information before it happens to stop it from happening. That only happens on TV.

"If there's one thing that's not cool to be in the streets, that's a snitch . . ."

I was in Barcelona with Eminem and G-Unit when Murder Inc. started a promotional campaign for Ja Rule's album. They got crazy and went on the radio like, "50's got an order of protection out against us"—like I need protection from Irv Gotti and Ja Rule. They were attempting to make themselves look tough because they call themselves "the Murderers." I'm hesitant to deal with the bullshit altercations that go on with music. It's some new shit, and I'm still learning a new way to handle everything. I'm used to dealing with problems on the up-and-up—the way it's supposed to be dealt with in the 'hood. When it's on, I can just go see these niggas. When the first shot is thrown in the 'hood, the second shot can be thrown back in the 'hood. But now that the first shot is thrown publicly, it makes it bad for me actually to return the shot. But these pussies use my hesitancy to their advantage and put it on their back, like they had anything to do with anything that's happened to me, even when they weren't involved: "Yeah, we did that." They start speaking French—we. But it wasn't them. Those niggas aren't a threat to anyone. They can rub elbows with niggas who may possibly do something, but that's all they can do.

I was ignoring them because they're inconsequential. People talk about this "long-running" beef, when I actually made a few songs about them five years ago and then ignored them. They started that campaign long before I had an album deal. It started when they felt my buzz in New York. It was an attempt to keep me from getting any money in the streets, even if I wasn't successful with my music. I wasn't making any money from the music business when they started spreading that shit, so it's like they were trying to kill my plan B. If there's one thing that it's not cool to be in the streets, it's a snitch. You sentence a nigga to death when you call him that.

CHAPTER 26

I think that my having a street-based situation and my lyrical content is what made them call me a snitch. They thought my music career wasn't going to take off, so they wanted to cut off my escape route. They didn't attack my music career because they didn't think anything was going to come of it—I was back in the 'hood with it. So when they called me a snitch in the 'hood, niggas in the 'hood started looking at me differently. Niggas who owed me money started acting like they didn't want to pay, which complicated my street situation.

Once I signed with Em and Dre, they got desperate and started talking out of the side of their mouth on the radio. When they did that, I was like, You know what? I'm sick of this shit. We flew straight from Barcelona to Detroit and went berserk in the studio. We did about sixteen freestyles and six songs in one night. We had something for every beat that Em played. He was looking at us like we weren't human. It was like, *This is it. No holds barred. We gon' kill them and let them know we're not backing down from nobody. If this is where you wanna take it, we're gonna take it there.*

That's when the dis records started coming in the street from me. I did it that way because I knew the music would stick around longer than the bullshit they said on the radio. A radio interview plays while you're there talking, but then when you leave, it's gone. The music that I put out gets played over and over and over.

I leave them alone now because they're not relevant. They'll never hurt anybody themselves. They're cowards, and for cowards it's all about who you can put yourself next to. A gangsta will always side up with a weak party who needs them for strength. That's because most gangstas haven't developed their talents. Instead, they take advantage of people who have talent through fear. The fear factor allows a weak artist to hang with gangstas, to make the stories he puts on a record sound real. If someone's whole gangsta backstory is a lie, he's going to try to make it look like it's real by standing next to someone who may have had those experiences. But that doesn't mean that you're down with gangstas. That just means you're getting extorted by gangstas.

"Every time I was in the newspaper, it was for some shit that didn't have anything to do with music . . ."

On New Year's Eve 2003, I was set to perform in the Copacabana nightclub in Manhattan. We were parked outside when the cops pulled up and told us we had to move the car. As soon as we drove around the corner, we heard sirens: *Whoop! Whoop! Whoop!* Cops everywhere. They said they saw a gun in the car, but I don't know how they saw a gun through a tinted window. They didn't "find" guns until after they "searched" the vehicle. Naturally, they tried to make like they were mine. Unfortunately for them, those were not my guns. Not that go-round. They ran us all through the system, and since Yayo had prior warrants he couldn't get bail. He had had those gun charges for a long time. When everything was about to pop for me, I told him, "You can leave now, but you might not be coming back to nothing." He had faith that I was going to blow up but wanted to help me finish putting the record out before he turned himself in. He stayed on the run until he was caught.

Before we had gotten arrested, I had parked my Hummer on 54th Street. When I came out the next morning, I figured that the car should be in the pound because it was parked by a meter. I went to the pound but the car wasn't there. What the fuck did they do with the car? The pound called the precinct and the cops told them that the car is in a new location. How did the car get moved? For what reason? What were they trying to do? Save me the trouble of a parking ticket because they like me so much? The only way it got moved is if the police physically got into the car and moved it. They took my keys when I got arrested so it was real easy for them to do whatever they wanted while I was being held. I figure they must've put something in there. I know they'd like to hear what the conversation is when we think tape recorders aren't rolling. I gave that car to my son's mom and I haven't been in it since then.

That incident got me back in the papers again: RAPPER 50 CENT AR-RESTED WITH GUNS. Every time I was in the newspaper, it was for some shit that didn't have anything to do with music. They had my picture in the paper next to some notorious heavyweights from the Queens drug game. That left a negative impression on people, since the things the papers said about me were never positive. And because the lyrical content of my records reflects the environment that I'm from, it all came together in people's minds: *50 Cent is a problem.* I'll be honest, I loved the free publicity. But controversy doesn't sell records—it just gets attention. Once I had the attention, I had to make sure the music could live up to the hype, because nothing sells more records than good music.

The major labels' system for selling records is that they'll put out a single and wait. If they really believe in the artist, they'll put out little posters with pretty pictures of the artist and take out some magazine ads. Then they'll drop another single, releasing an album with the second single. The problem is the consumer still doesn't know the artist, and he's not sure if the album is any good. Someone could buy the album because he likes the first two singles, but that's a gamble—especially if only one other song on it is any good. I think people are sick of being punked for sixteen dollars.

But I had generated so much interest on the mix-tape circuit that people knew what to expect from my album when it came out. I treated the mix-tape circuit like a chemistry set—I got to see what the consumers would react to and get excited about and what they wouldn't. I had to study so I could know how to pick music. I listened to probably 40,000 beats putting together my album. I listened to a lot of unknown producers. I may have gotten about five or six hundred CDs, if not more than that, and they all had about thirty or forty beats on them. I sifted through them to find the beats that were hot to me. It didn't matter to me who produced the record. I feel like beat CDs should come blank with no name on it, so people would pick a beat because it's the right beat, not because *this producer* made it. A lot of times artists get blinded by who made a beat: because the Neptunes made it, it's a hit; or Timbaland; or Dre, or whoever. I think the consistency that Dr. Dre, the Neptunes, and Timbaland have had with making hits make artists pick beats from those that may not be the right song for the artist. It might still be a hit song, but it wasn't *their* hit song, it wasn't the song for them at that point.

When I sit and listen to beats, even with Dre, there's certain beats that got my name written on them. It's not until after we did one or two songs that he got in tune with what I liked, and then he knew what to play for me. When he got in the studio and he got comfortable working with me, then he had shit that was *for* me. He had specifics in his head that he knew I wanted after he heard me rhyme to his beats. We did this one song for my album, "Heat." That beat was hanging around Dre's camp for a while. It was around and they didn't know exactly what to do to make it what it should be. And then he gave it to me, and we did that song in about an hour.

My determination to turn out an album full of dope singles, my discriminating ear for what's hot, and my experience with the mixtape circuit paid off big-time. My album *Get Rich or Die Tryin'* was illegally downloaded more than three hundred thousand times before it went on sale. It was getting bootlegged so much that we had to push up the release date. But get this: It still sold 872,000 copies in the first week, and it wasn't even a full week. The second week, when an album usually drops off by 35 percent (according to *Billboard*), *Get Rich* hit 822,000 in record sales. My record showed almost no drop. A lot of executives and some of the public couldn't understand how a new artist could go platinum in just two weeks. Their thinking was, Come on. Nobody knows the guy. How could he be selling so many records? But my hard-core fans and my boys understood. *Get Rich* represented so much more than a number on a chart; it represented my struggle and determination to push through all the negativity, all the roadblocks. I had such a hard time getting my product out on the street and through the majors that I poured all my personality, all my soul, all of myself into it—and I think people could tell. That's what they responded to. With *Get Rich*, I really put myself out there. And I think it became evident that *Get Rich or Die Tryin'* wasn't just an album title; it was my mission.

I am truly blessed. And I remind myself every day that if I'm in a good space now, it's because I been in a bad space for so long before. I don't consider myself a role model, because I think a role model should be speaking and saying something positive all the time. That ain't me. But my story has to be an inspiration to people that's from the bottom, people that's from the same walks of life I'm from. I'm proof that success is possible. They can look at me and say, "I know *I* could do *this*, because *he* did *that*."

I'm feeling my new pop star status, too. I guess because I'm popular, that makes me a pop star. It's great. Every artist wants to be a pop star, no matter what angle they take. Pop stars have all the fun and get all the endorsements. I probably have the hardest album ever to sell pop numbers. If you say I'm pop that doesn't mean I'm the same as *NYSNC. It just means that people embrace *the music*. And that's the object: to have people embrace the music. I just put a different spin on it because I'm gangsta about mine. When I see myself on the cover of a magazine and it says something like, "Why He's Your Favorite Gangsta," or "The Hunted Man," or some other shit, I eat that shit up. I think it's more interesting than the usual garbage.

Even with all the stuff out there about me, I don't feel any more hunted than I ever did. Everybody's got somebody who don't like them. I dislike some people, too. But it's just about what makes sense and what doesn't make sense to me right now. I really don't care who dislikes me or why. I don't waste energy on that mess. I got to be about mine. That might sound selfish, but it's real. I'm not going to be the asshole that got in this position and still jumped out the window 'cause he couldn't make the pieces fit. I don't want to be the same way as I was out in the street. But sometimes I feel like that shit so much. Old habits die real hard. Just 'cause you change a man's surroundings doesn't mean that you change the man. Good times can mess with you just as much as bad times can, if you get caught out there.

In my case, everything good that could happen to me, happened all at once. Here I am the same dude from Jamaica, Queens, I was a few years back, except now everybody knows me and I have all this cash. *Get Rich or Die Tryin'* sold eleven million copies worldwide. I got a deal with Reebok for the G-Unit sneaker, I got the G-Unit clothing line about to pop, a Vitamin Water called Formula 50, and a movie project in development. It's crazy. I have the means to do just about anything I've ever wanted to do and some things I never thought of. It's pretty fly, but it's dangerous, too. I see why so many cats just lose it and get real caught up, 'cause *nothing* is off limits to you. Without discipline, that's a pretty dangerous place to be.

That's exactly why I'm trying to give back. Deep down I do know it's not all about 50—no matter what the groupies or the execs say. Groupies ain't picky. They change loyalties like I change drawers. And executives . . . those same executives wasn't even trying to hear me back in the day. Pretty much only Eminem and Dre showed me any love up front. As for them other fools, I know that the day I stop being hot is the day I get dropped. So I'm trying to do my part, while I still got it to do. That's why I formed the G-Unity Foundation. That's my heart right there. Its whole purpose is to give real financial support to groups who are doing something in the community. Most nonprofits in the 'hood don't usually get the cash they need to make an impact 'cause nobody is checking for them. G-Unity Foundation wants to change that. We want to make sure that we get money to the people who need it the most, the ones who are really doing the work, the ones who are really going to use it to help the community.

Being able to help people in the 'hood is just one of the good things about having a gang of loot. But like I said before, I'm still pretty much the same person I was before the success. I don't think anybody takes that into consideration except the police. That's why they follow me everywhere I go and watch everything I do. They definitely have their outlook on who I am. They're going, Now that he has the money, he could do anything at this point. And then he's got people that don't have nothing to lose that hate him. The people that dislike me have nothing to lose, so they can act like a fool. For me that means more bulletproof vehicles, bullet-proof vests, tighter security, and shit like that 'cause a nigga might decide to bust a shot just to boost his reputation. Even if he ain't hit nobody, it's great for him in the 'hood. To say you shot *at* 50. Great. Your stock goes up like a motherfucker. It's stupid as hell. But it's true.

And it's more likely to happen at home than it is anywhere else. Home is the last place you get your love. I realize that now. You can't show love to a person that you grew up with that you feel like, "Oh, this nigga thinks he's ill now because he raps. I remember when he didn't have this or when he didn't have that and he was like this." That's all ex-homies could do is remember the past. But those memories are enough to make them try to take you down a peg or two—or take you out. That's one of the reasons that I'm glad to be out the 'hood. People ask me all the time if I miss home. Fuck no. I'm glad to be gone. I spent twenty-six years trying to get out of that motherfucker. Let me spend a few years somewhere else.

I hate going to perform in New York City now. Like I said, cops follow me everywhere I go. The time I came back from doing *Saturday Night Live,* there were two cop cars full of cops. *Full,* like they didn't have room in another cop car. They rode behind us everywhere we went. I was like, "Yo man, take me to the hotel. Put me up. Now!" Why? Because the time before when these niggas was behind me, and they followed me from the radio station to Sony Studios where I was doing something with DMX, when we left that studio to go to the Copacabana, we went to jail instead.

What can I say? I don't pick my fights with the law or anybody else. I just end up in them. Some of this shit, you don't go, "Well, I'ma go to the club tonight and start a fight." Nah. It just happens. If you knew it was coming, you'd stay your ass at home just to avoid the confrontation, be-cause nowadays if you get into a fistfight, you kinda hope to lose. Because if you win, nine out of ten times, you've got to worry about the nigga com-ing back to tear your head off. Yeah, it's crazy when I go back home. The only time I'm glad to go to New York is when no one knows where I'm gonna be ahead of time. Then I can enjoy myself without all the drama. Even though I don't like going to NYC announced, I never forget exactly where I just came from and who helped me get where I'm at now.

I just got in the rap game and I don't want to turn my blessings into something negative that I can't come back from. I believe in a higher power. I believe in right and wrong. I believe in God. I believe everything about the church is cool, but everybody's not there in the right spirit. If I was in the church and said the things that I say on my records, I wouldn't be okay to be there. The odds of Yolanda Adams doing a record with 50 Cent are very slim.

Even if the lyrical content on that record was good, what is going to be said before and after that on my other records? My outlook on the church is that it's a positive thing. I think it's a place where you go to be reminded of your morals and realign yourself with how you're supposed to live. Then you got Monday through Saturday to put it into effect, until you make it to the next Sunday where you can reestablish it in your head again. It's the same thing when you're on the street. A lot of times, you watch the same films over and over again to remind you of your code. You watch *Scarface,* you watch *Casino,* you watch gangster films a lot in the 'hood. I think that inspires you to bust a head or to pull your pistol out when the time comes. You condition yourself to that shit through the visuals and what you listen to and everything else. As quiet as it's kept, it's a brain-washing process.

But not everybody gets it. A lot of rappers will stand in front of you and tell you some shit they know damn well they didn't experience. They'll stand in front of you and spit their rhymes like they mean it, but they don't know what they're talking about. With me, 90 percent of my music is real, and only about 10 percent of it I'll embellish. I'll expand shit just because that's the creative part of the music. But you can check my record about what I say and you'll see that most of the shit that I say adds up. I may change the name, the place, or some small details, but people that know the truth can go, "This part fits, but we don't know exactly who it is now 'cause he didn't tell us that part." I use real shit.

I wouldn't have anything to write about if I didn't use my own experiences. You're being unfair if you tell me to come up with rhymes and not use what I came from, to put no part of me or anything that I've been through in the music. If I don't write about what's going on with me or what's taking place in the 'hood, I ain't got nothing to say. The day 50 can't be real, that's the day I say, "Thank you for all your support, it's been a pleasure"—and I leave.

When artists get spoiled that's when they start slipping. They start believing their own hype. They get to a place where they think that they shouldn't have to be out performing anymore. That ain't me. The way I see it, regular people go to work every day from nine to five, picking up boxes, doing hard labor, picking up swing shifts, and you're telling me all I have to do is get on stage for forty-five minutes? Fuck that. I'm getting out on that motherfucker. I need to be there every night. It's a luxury to be in this business. I get to be in a different city every night. I've been touring since three months before my first album came out *and* getting paid for it. When I look at how much I get paid now and compare it to what I was making standing on the corner of the block, for the hours I was clocking, it's no contest. What do you mean, *I need a rest?* No. I don't need a rest. I'll rest in between shows, tour dates, and video shoots. Because you know what? On the corner I didn't need a rest. I didn't even stop sometimes to change my clothes, because I was grinding. There were times I slept outside when I was hustling. I was just out there on the bench like everybody else. It's summertime, it's hot, I ain't gone home last night. I didn't quit in my old business and I'm not going to quit in my new business either.

Ask any hustler and they will all say the same thing: "If there is money to be made, then I'm gonna be the one to make it." A hustler's attitude is, "they gon' get it from somewhere, so it might as well be from me. I may as well make them ends." And "it" can be anything. Sometimes it's drugs. But it can be music, clothes, drink, cars, or even hamburgers. People think that a hustler's mentality is confined to the ghetto, to pimps and dealers. But that ain't true. America was founded on a hustler's mentality. All the big names from way back started out pushin' something. And from what I understand, theirs wasn't always legal either. The list of modern-day hustlers I personally know reads like a who's who in the music game. Jay-Z and Master P had been real to the game on the streets. Diddy might not have been slangin',' but when you read about his early days at Uptown, under Andre Harrell, it's clear that my boy was grindin.' All of them niggas just took their grind and transitioned it into something else. They can pretty much make whatever they do work, because they stay hungry. For them, enough is never enough, it's just the beginning.

What's interesting to me is that I see in Master P the same thing that I see in Jay-Z, that I see in Diddy, that I know is in me. All of them are still hustling. Like, Fuck you, pay me. That shit is still there. And they ain't trying to hide it. And if what you got to say is not about that, then as far as they're concerned, you ain't saying nothing. I respect that.

On the flip side, some people do music as a hobby, but it's more than that to me. For me, music is everything. It's my opportunity to get away from the 'hood, to make a better life for my son, to do everything I ever wanted to do. And I'm putting my all into it. You can't meet your goals by accident. That's like thinking you're going to hit the lottery, but you're not buying a ticket. I have to treat this like I treated the block. It's a damn shame, but I have to internalize things in a negative way to understand them. I look at things from a street mentality because that's what I understand. That's the only way I can know for sure how to play things. All the other shit, I'm still learning. I never had a job in my life. And even if my music career hadn't taken off, I don't think I would have ever had a job, because working nine to five is a trap. If I couldn't do something to invest in and do other things as an entrepreneur, then I would have died in the hood doing what I did. But now I've made it this far and I'm happy. Like I say in my rhymes, *If I die today, I'm happy how my life turned out.* I have gone from pieces to weight in more ways than one.

The thing is this: all of the money, all of the success—none of it is going to keep me alive longer than I'm meant to be. But the ICU is finished with 50 Cent. They're through seeing me under any circumstances. The way I see it, even a nigga like me ain't no accident. Like I said before, I believe in God. I didn't survive being shot nine times for nothing. I didn't claw my way out of the 'hood just 'cause it was something to do. I know I've got a purpose—a reason for being on this planet. I don't think I've done everything I'm supposed to do yet. But I do know this: I ain't going nowhere 'til I've done it all.